Vicarious learning is critical because none of us have enough time to make all the mistakes we need to make to learn all the lessons we need to learn, and some mistakes are simply too costly to learn firsthand. *Unleader* will accelerate the journey of vicarious learning in the most important leadership textbook any of us will ever have, the Bible. Don't get in a hurry to finish this book; soak in each chapter and let these practical principles from the case study of Saul and David transform your leadership from the inside out.

Steve Moore
President and CEO, The Mission Exchange
Author of Who Is My Neighbor? Being a Good Samaritan in a
    Connected World

Christian leadership involves values or traits that you may not always hear about in the hallways of corporate America. *Unleader* speaks to the very essence of how God expects us to lead. This book cuts through the noise of leadership . . . and drives you to your knees.

Our Western culture says it values leadership, but mostly we value leaders copying other successful leaders. *Unleader* is a refreshing look at what it means to truly be a leader.

A crucial part of leading is asking the right questions. *Unleader* forces the reader to ask the hard questions and then explores the biblical solutions.

Brian Mosley
President
RightNow & Bluefish TV, Plano,

D1364194

As a younger leader who has been ....)r ten years, I can say Jane authentically lives out the servant leadership that she describes in this book. Jane's devotion to Christ is revealed in these pages as she unfolds the essence of leadership—the heart. *Unleader* challenges those in leadership to consider prayerfully how their leadership brings joy or grief to the heart of God. May Jane's words be used by God to encourage younger leaders to lead out of vibrant relationship with Christ, enabling us to extend the kingdom of God on earth his way!

Dr. Leslie Neal Segraves
Cofounder and Executive Director
10/40 Connections, Inc., Chattanooga, TN

I just finished reading Jane Overstreet's marvelous book, *Unleader*. Rather than picking out a few proof-text verses to make her point, Jane invites us into the biblical story in order to let God walk into our stories as leaders. The insights found in *Unleader* bring invaluable practical lessons for leaders in all circumstances. But more importantly, in these pages, Jane paints a vision of servant leadership that is engaging and powerful.

Bill Tibert
Senior Pastor
Covenant Presbyterian Church, Colorado Springs, CO

As a leader you will from time to time feel that you are crossing a line that you didn't really mean to cross; it just happens. If you cross it enough times you may no longer see the line and won't recognize from where you have fallen. This book's insightful analysis of the lives of Saul and David will help you see those lines and get back on course to be a person after God's own heart.

Through the lens of this astute study of Saul and David's lives, I was challenged to examine myself, and I would genuinely recommend leaders to do so. I plan to use it for group discussion with other leaders.

Dr. Raju Abraham
Neurologist, Medical Director
Kachhwa Christian Hospital Transformational Ministries, Uttar
    Pradesh, India

UNLEADER

THE SURPRISING QUALITIES OF A VALUABLE LEADER

JANE OVERSTREET

Transforming lives through God's Word

Transforming lives through God's Word

Biblica provides God's Word to people through translation, publishing and Bible engagement in Africa, Asia Pacific, Europe, Latin America, Middle East, and North America. Through its worldwide reach, Biblica engages people with God's Word so that their lives are transformed through a relationship with Jesus Christ.

Biblica Publishing
We welcome your questions and comments.

1820 Jet Stream Drive, Colorado Springs, CO 80921 USA
www.Biblica.com

Unleader
ISBN-13: 978-1-60657-039-5

Copyright © 2011 by Jane Overstreet

13 12 11 / 6 5 4 3 2

Published in 2011 by Biblica Publishing

A catalog record for this book is available through the Library of Congress.

Printed in the United States of America

Contents

Foreword

As you pick up this book, you may be thinking exactly what I was thinking when I wrote it—what the world does not need is one more book on leadership! Well, at least we agree on that!

So why did I write this book anyway? While the world truly does not need one more book from a famous leader telling us why we should follow his model of leadership, we still need better leaders. And leaders need tools to help them keep growing and I believe this book can be such a tool.

The world is hungry for humble, godly servant leaders who grasp why God has given them position and power. Leadership too often degenerates into being about us, our reputations, and our agendas, but there is nothing further from the heart and mind of God than these selfish strivings.

Leadership is never about us. Instead, these roles of leadership are given to us in order for us to enable and strengthen local expressions of the body of Christ and then see that body reach out and bring the healing power of the gospel into the broken world around us. That is God's intention and what the world so desperately needs.

In order for this book to work as a learning tool for you, take the time to read and quietly reflect on these stories of Saul and David from the Bible, comparing your experience with theirs. Also try using it as an excuse to gather with two or more others to read these stories and reflect together so that you help each other grow. Doing these simple things will give the Holy Spirit room to speak to your heart and show you areas of your leadership that need to grow and change. He loves it when we let him do that.

May this book help you grow in using your leadership as he intended. May your leadership—and my leadership—bring God joy, just like David's did.

Does My Leadership Look More like Saul's or David's?

I will never forget sitting in a friend's house in West Africa late one afternoon and listening to a small group of local leaders discuss politics. It was still quite hot out, though the sun was setting. The chairs were overstuffed and dusty, but thankfully very soft. It had been a long day of dialogue and teaching on integrity, and though I was tired and ready to rest, these leaders were still rapidly processing. As I sank gratefully into one of those soft chairs, I wanted to close my eyes; yet the conversation quickly grabbed my attention.

"Do you really think it is possible he could get elected?" one man continued.

"Oh, for sure, but then he would just succumb to 'the disease' like everyone else does," answered a second man.

The first speaker laughed bitterly. "Yes, I suppose you are right. It is impossible to get elected here and not be corrupt, isn't it?"

"No, no, you are wrong," piped up a softer voice from the corner. "Remember Thomas Sankaroa?" Suddenly the whole room went quiet and heads lowered.

"Who was Sankaroa?" I couldn't help interrupting.

"A former president," came the quick response. "He was amazing and stood for what was right for the two weeks he was in power. He was pure and so determined to make a difference. But then he was assassinated because he wouldn't give in to the military bosses. We all thought he could bring some positive change, but of course he was just killed."

"What do *you* think?" All heads turned toward me. "Do you think it is possible for us to have a righteous leader, a good leader, someone who will do something besides line his own pockets, pay his own people, and build a villa in Europe?!" they demanded.

"Well, of, of, uhhh, . . . of course it is possible." I stammered a little as the temperature in the room seemed to noticeably rise and the perspiration streamed off my face. I was desperately hoping that the randomly rotating fan would soon point back in my direction. "Really, it is possible," I continued, "but it will probably have to be one of you, . . . because who besides a follower of Jesus could hope to have the character and integrity necessary to withstand the pressure of corruption long enough to bring lasting change?"

A long silence followed, and then there were deep sighs around the room, followed by much more conversation as the leaders present contemplated what would happen if they were handed that much power. Could they withstand the temptations? Would they be any different from so many others?

And what about you? What would your leadership look like if you were suddenly handed more power? How do you think you would respond to that situation? Would your leadership be an example of righteousness and justice, or would you give in to the temptations that power always presents. A simple way to answer that question is to evaluate what your leadership looks like right now.

Leadership Development Is a Lifelong Process

One of my observations after more than twenty years of working with Christian leaders around the world is that usually our leadership looks more like the culture in which we live, than like the culture and values of the kingdom of God. This is because we automatically lead as we have been led or seen others lead. We replicate what we have experienced.

Every culture puts a slightly different mask on those qualities of leadership it holds dear, and all our cultures are terribly broken. Perhaps some are significantly worse than others, but none of them accurately reflect God's values. The values of the kingdom of God are countercultural to every earthly culture.

God's values also go against our human nature. Justice, goodness, dying to self, humility—none of these come naturally to any of us. That is why becoming a leader who pleases God and brings him joy is impossible apart from our growing in relationship with God. Only this enables us to deepen our understanding and practice of the things that bring him pleasure. We have to continue imbibing his character so that it impacts our leadership decisions and actions. This makes Christian leadership development inherently a lifelong process.

This is a book written to help leaders bring God joy. It doesn't matter where you are in your leadership journey—there is always more to learn. If you have been the leader of a large ministry for forty years—there is so much more to learn. Or if you have led one small group and you are still in college—there is so much more to learn.

At age fifty I remember complaining to one of my mentors that the older I get, the more I realize how little I know. I had always hoped that it would be the other way around, that I would somehow finally "arrive"; but instead I just realize the vastness of all there is to know and how little of it I do know! His response was classic: "To realize how little you know is the beginning of wisdom."

I hope this book helps you grow in wisdom. It is designed just for that, to let you practically evaluate and assess your own leadership and then take steps to grow. It is not about judging someone else's leadership, however good or bad it might be. The problem with taking that approach is that it is rarely productive. Focusing on others' mistakes can make us bitter, and it keeps us from assessing and changing ourselves.

Instead, this book is completely committed to helping *you* grow. By asking you some simple and straightforward questions, I hope you will be challenged to look squarely in the mirror and honestly evaluate where you are succeeding and falling short as a leader. Once you clearly see where the gap is between what your leadership looks like and what it should be, then you can ask God to help you take steps to change. I pray that is what will happen as you read and study this book.

Why Ask This Question?

Does your leadership look more like Saul's or David's? As the title to this chapter indicates, this is the central question to begin this journey of self-discovery and evaluation. Of course I am referring to the first two kings of Israel, whose stories are told in the books of 1 and 2 Samuel in the Old Testament.

Can the ancient stories of two Old Testament kings be relevant for us today? Is it possible for a book based on a study of these two characters to be worthwhile reading for today's leaders?

There is no question that leadership development is one of the most popular subjects of our time. You notice it by glancing at airport bookstores where entire shelves are dedicated to the newest one hundred titles on the subject. Academic institutions that thirty years ago did not have a single course on leadership now offer several degree tracks related to the subject. The business world has created an entire industry in response to this interest, with a vast array of experts, consultants, executive development groups, and institutions purely dedicated to leadership training.

And if we know one thing about leaders, it is that they do not have enough time. In our frantic world, time is one of the most precious resources for leaders, often more precious than money. Even if leaders are interested in reading and studying about leadership, does a study about two ancient leaders warrant the limited time and attention span of today's leaders?

For two very good reasons the answer to these questions is a resounding yes. First of all, human nature has essentially been the same since time began. For example, the first issues faced in the garden of Eden between a man and a woman are not that different from those faced by any couple today. For them one problem was the "blame game." When God asked Adam what he had done by eating the fruit given to him by the serpent, his answer is essentially, "She made me do it!" Sound familiar?

People have been self-centered, focused on their own interests and reputations, and living in fear of authority ever since sin entered the world. Therefore, real stories about real leaders from any era and any culture are relevant to us today.

A second reason that the stories of Saul and David are instructive for us is because the Bible is full of stories about God intervening in the lives of ordinary people. God is the same yesterday, today, and forever. His dealings with the children of Israel in the time of Saul and David are time bound in their details but universal in their principles and implications. Therefore, there is much to learn from these ancient stories of people trying to lead others while relating to the almighty and everlasting God of the universe.

The Bible is the Word of God, and God is the source of all truth. So even if you are a leader in the business or political realm, you will find that the best leadership principles are biblical in origin. Often secular authors of books on leadership do not recognize their principles as biblical, but in fact they are.

Think about it for a minute. "Level 5 leadership" as described by Jim Collins in his book *Good to Great* is a wonderful description of the Christlike leader. How about Patrick Lencioni's book on team building? Guilty again, it is full of tremendous biblical principles. The list is really endless because the Bible is the Word of God and God is the source of all truth. If you have read many good books on leadership, you'll think of many of your own examples.

The Bhutanese Refugee Relevance Test Is Key

One of my early experiences in leadership development taught me the difference between culturally bound leadership theories and those that are timeless truth. This lesson took place on the far eastern plains of Nepal with Christian leaders from the Bhutanese refugee population there. What were Bhutanese refugees doing in eastern Nepal? Believe me, they were asking themselves the same question!

As so many stories do, this one begins with a bad leader—in this case, the king of Bhutan. He forced a large band of Bhutanese Christians and other ethnic minorities to leave Bhutan many years ago as a form of ethnic cleansing. They were given only brief notice and literally marched out of the country with whatever they could carry. Through enormous suffering and great hardship they crossed the border into India but were not allowed to stop there because of concerns from the local government. So they were forced to march into Nepal. Once they crossed the Nepal border, they were finally allowed to stop, and enormous refugee camps were established for these people.

When I arrived at these camps, they had been in existence for years. Despite continuous lobbying by international agencies, these wanderers were essentially in a no man's land. They were not allowed to legally work in Nepal, they were not allowed to return to Bhutan, and they had no reason for hope for the future.

Yet, they were resourceful people. They had created churches within the camps that were wonderful examples of godly fellowships. The camps themselves were extremely clean and well managed, almost like lovely towns in many respects. They had set up schools and microbusinesses out of almost nothing. Those businesses were so successful that the local Nepali community was regularly involved in trading with them.

The local Christian leaders invited us in to provide teaching in integrity and effectiveness—and frankly I could not figure out what *we* had to teach them. Slowly, over multiple cups of hot tea, we began opening up stories of leaders in Scripture and learned together the lessons of leadership that were there for all of us.

Although I had come laden with curriculum, I quickly learned that unless it was truly biblically based it was irrelevant. Some of the teaching I had brought with me was too culturally bound, steeped in Western examples and not of much value to these leaders.

At that moment, the "Bhutanese Refugee Relevance Test" was born. The test is this: if leadership development lessons that I develop as an American make sense to Bhutanese refugees and are applicable in their daily leadership, they are clearly universal truths.

The leadership lessons that we are going to look at in this book pass the Bhutanese Refugee Relevance Test. That is, they are timeless, universal truths that we find in biblical stories about leaders interacting with God and with their followers. They are stories that we can learn from today and apply as we daily lead others.

Current Challenges Are Timeless Challenges

One of my roles gives me the opportunity to serve on the Leadership Development Working Group (LDWG) for the Lausanne Movement. The Lausanne Movement was birthed at a conference on world evangelization held in the city of Lausanne, Switzerland, in 1974. There leaders from around the globe met together to learn from each other about what was happening in evangelism globally and to be encouraged to reach more of the world with the good news of the gospel of Jesus Christ.

Today that same concept continues in the form of the Lausanne Movement. As part of the movement, various working groups have been formed to correspond, consult, and work together on issues that deeply impact the success or failure of efforts aimed at world evangelization. The condition of Christian leaders is clearly one of those issues.

In fact, leadership development has been one of the most frequently cited needs among Christian leaders for the last twenty years. When leaders are surveyed about what they believe are the key issues holding back the growth of the church, lack of effective leadership development always ranks very high.

During 2008–2009 the LDWG surveyed the realm of challenges relating to the intersection between leadership development and world evangelization and discovered two areas that seemed to stand out as critical ones where this particular group could uniquely make a contribution. Those were (1) to define Christ-centered leadership and (2) to describe what is most effective in building Christ-centered leaders.

Rather than do this through a purely academic approach or alternatively through pooling our own opinions, the LDWG launched a survey process that was primarily web based to ask Christian leaders globally what they thought about these issues.

More than a thousand Christian leaders responded from across seven continents. Of those surveyed there was a wide range of ages, types of leadership experience, and quantities of leadership experience. Approximately one-third of those surveyed were women. The survey was also conducted in five languages to try to get a wide range of opinions. (For a detailed description of respondents to this survey, see the results of questions 27–32 of the survey in the appendix.)

We found out a great deal about how these leaders would define Christlike leadership. In fact, across the cultures, languages, and experiences, the responses were hauntingly similar. They overwhelmingly responded that the top three characteristics that describe Christ-centered leadership, in order of ranking, are the following:

- Integrity, authenticity, excellent character
- Servant's heart, humble
- Spiritually mature, hears God's voice, holy and prayerful

Lower on the list came the following:

- Excellent people management skills and ability to discern and develop the gifts of others
- Biblical knowledge, theologically sound
- Compassionate, good listener, more oriented to people than accomplishing the task

There was also a disturbing outcome from the survey. Christian leaders said that too many Christian leaders fail. When asked to describe their worst experiences working under leaders and what characteristics those poor leaders had, they said the following:

- Prideful, always right, and always the big boss
- Lack of integrity, untrustworthy
- Harsh, uncaring, refused to listen, critical

Slightly lower on the list were the following:

- Inability to manage people and enable them to work together
- Spiritually immature, no evidence of holiness or prayerfulness

Keep in mind these descriptors were not used to describe non-Christian leaders, but rather Christian leaders, or those who said they were Christian.

Leaders in our survey were also asked a similar question in a different way, but the results were strikingly similar. They were asked the question, "From the list below choose up to five of the most pressing issues facing Christian leaders in your nation."

The most frequent response to that question was "Personal pride," followed by "Integrity." Then two hundred votes further down the list were "Spiritual warfare," "Corruption," and "Lack of infrastructure (training)."

This emphasis on the issue of personal pride should be surprising when compared with other issues facing leaders, like poverty and corruption. But on closer reflection this points out the vast damage done by the disease of "big boss" leadership, which is the very antithesis of the servant leadership style of Jesus.

"Big boss" leadership says, "Since I have the leadership position, I can do whatever I want to do, and you have to do whatever I say because you are under me." It can come in a much more subtle form than that, but no matter what cultural spin it comes with, it is still an ugly, self-serving abomination to God and completely perverts what God intended leaders to be.

I have often thought of the example I heard once while in Uganda. There a friend was teaching about leadership and asked the audience what the word was for *leadership* in the local language. The group responded with the local word for *leadership*, and my friend asked for a literal translation. Quickly came the response: "It means 'to eat.'"

Puzzled I listened more closely as the discussion continued. "Why does it mean 'to eat'?" my friend asked.

"Oh," came the response, "because when you are the leader, you can eat anything you want, and no one can stop you."

"Oh," he said, "now you see why our culture has a problem trying to demonstrate Christlike servant leadership. It goes against the very core of our understanding of the role of the leader." And so it is in almost every culture.

Christlike leadership is a challenge because it is inherently countercultural in every setting. It goes against the very essence of our selfish human nature. It is antithetical to what is natural. (For a more complete understanding of the results of the survey, see the appendix.)

What is true about the failure of leaders today has an eerie similarity to what was true in the days of Saul and David. One of the things you will notice as you go through this study is that the issues pointed out by more than a thousand leaders across seven continents in five languages are the same issues that caused God to say that he was sorry he ever chose Saul to lead. On the positive side, they are the things that David got right and that caused God to call him a leader after his own heart.

How Should You Evaluate Your Leadership?

Human nature causes us to regularly compare ourselves to others. There is constant pressure to determine whether we measure up to those we see as successful. Often we are asking ourselves whether we are good leaders. Are we great leaders? Are we the best? Are we successful? How do we know?

Many leadership books are especially unhelpful when it comes to evaluating ourselves because they are written by famous leaders about their personal experiences, with the underlying suggestion that if you do what they did you too can become successful. You too can become the top executive of a large corporation or the senior pastor of a megachurch. They share with you their experiences so that you can become rich and famous too, even if they don't say that directly.

And, in fact, we read them because we want to become rich and famous. Bigger is better. If our church or ministry grows, then we are successful. If our name becomes well known, we will be happier. The more things we collect, the more fulfilled we will be. At some level most of us have bought into these lies that this is what great leadership is about—ourselves.

When others measure our leadership, whether they are executive consultants or the people in the pews, it may be somewhat more helpful. They usually look at a variety of standards. Depending on the role we are playing, they will ask if our organization or church is growing. Are we having a great impact? Did we meet our goals last year? Are our revenues higher this year than they were last year? Were our revenues higher than our expenses? Did the shareholders get the rewards they expected? Have we been promoted to a position with more responsibility, authority, and salary?

There are lots of ways to measure the quality and effectiveness of our leadership. And while some of these are valid standards depending on our role, many are ultimately irrelevant. Too often we have misunderstood what successful leadership is all about. We do not know which standard to use for evaluation.

Let's Consider the Only Standard That Matters

When measuring performance, the only standard that truly matters to a follower of Jesus is what God thinks of our leadership. That is it. That is all. Does our leadership bring God joy, or does it bring him great sadness? That is truly all that matters. It all comes down to that.

When I think about standards of success, I often think about Aunt Hildreth, who passed away many years ago. Besides being my elderly auntie, she was also my Sunday school teacher for at least five years, from the time I entered the nursery at church until I turned about nine years of age. She was utterly kind, selfless, never sought position, but instead faithfully loved on generation after generation of snotty-nosed children.

She didn't just change a thousand diapers and feed us snacks while we sat around the little wooden tables in the basement of the church; she taught each one of us to love Jesus. She told us Bible stories and made them exciting. She held us and listened to our concerns and taught us to pray about each problem. She made sure that each Sunday school classroom had what it needed to successfully teach the gospel.

She recruited other volunteer teachers and mentored them in how to care for young children. She often recruited teenagers to work with the children and then sat and listened to them when they needed an adult to care. She probably never thought of herself as a leader, but of course she was. She was a force within the local church that ensured that hundreds of children came to a saving knowledge of Jesus and were discipled. She faithfully carried out the tasks that God called her to do. If we measured her by standards of this world, she would not have scored very high. Yet I am sure that her life and leadership brought God great joy.

I also think of the pastors in rural India—Orissa, for instance—who have been martyred for their faith in recent years. Were their churches growing? Did they have great impact? Did they meet their goals last year? Were their revenues higher than their expenses? Did they get regularly promoted to positions with more responsibility, authority, and salary? They probably failed most of those contemporary tests of success. Yet I am sure that God welcomed them into heaven with open arms, saying, "Well done, my good and faithful servants." According to God's standards, they were outstandingly successful leaders.

As we study together the lives and leadership styles of Saul and David in this book, I hope you will see this truth clearly. Measuring ourselves by any standard other than what God thinks of our leadership is at best irrelevant and at worst sinful.

Do you have any idea how your leadership affects God? How has he measured your success as a leader? Do your life and leadership cause him grief as Saul's did, or do they somehow bring joy to the heart of God as David's did?

Too frequently we lose perspective in the frantic day-to-day grind of leadership and fail to ask these important questions. We get confused as to which standards matter and which are merely ir-relevant symptoms. We lose our way.

So I want to invite you to stop and take a little time out of your important and busy schedule. Steal away a bit from the storms of daily life and responsibility, and reflect on the stories of Saul and David with me. Their stories will inform your story. Their failures and successes will help you evaluate your own leadership. And their experiences will help you remember which standard actually matters.

In the chapters that follow, you will have the opportunity to wrestle with five fundamental questions. By grappling with each of these, you will have the chance to arrive at an accurate conclusion about whether your leadership looks more like Saul's or David's, whether it brings God pleasure or causes God grief. Those questions are the following:

1. Do I fear people more than God?
2. Do I "use up" people under my leadership, or do I build up and enable them?
3. Do I put my interests first (greed and self-preservation) or God's interests first?
4. Do I lead with integrity?
5. Do I let people get close enough to really love me?

I pray that studying Saul's story and David's story while asking these questions will impact you. I pray that it will help you separate yourself from your own broken cultural standards and refocus on a biblical standard. I pray that it will enable you to hold up a mir-ror to your own leadership and answer these questions honestly for yourself.

Like my friends in the story from West Africa at the beginning of this chapter, sometimes we lose hope that good Christlike leader-ship is possible. But it is important to remember that we have many biblical examples that show us that even in the most difficult cultures and settings it is possible to please God. No matter how large your leadership role or how small, it is critical to ask God, "O Lord, do I bring you joy through my leadership, or do I bring you sorrow? Does my leadership look more like Saul's or David's?

Questions for Reflection:

- What is the ultimate standard for your leadership? What is your goal? Is your goal to bring God joy? How might that idea change your day-to-day activities?
- Do you believe that the main challenges of your leadership today bear any resemblance to the issues of leaders thousands of years ago?

Setting the Stage

Before we move into tackling the five questions listed at the end of the last chapter, I would like to set the stage for these stories of Saul and David, because it is in setting the stage that several disturbing realities become clear. And it is important to understand these events in order to grasp the meaning these stories hold for us today.

So let's explore three background pieces. First of all, we will examine the concept that the choosing of an earthly king in Israel was a tragedy about rejecting God. Second, we want to get to know Samuel as the key player, Christ figure, and godly leadership model in the beginning of these stories. And third, it will be important to recognize that many myths about leadership break down as it becomes clear that Saul and David had so much in common that their stories are almost identical in many respects, yet their lives ended so differently.

God Is Rejected by His People

Let us begin with the first issue raised, that the choosing of an earthly king in Israel was a tragedy about the people of Israel rejecting God.

We have to ask ourselves, Did God ever intend for his people to have a king? Certainly that doesn't seem to be true as you read through 1 Samuel 8:1–8.

> When Samuel grew old, he appointed his sons as Israel's leaders. The name of his firstborn was Joel and the name of his second was Abijah, and they served at Beersheba. But his sons did not follow his ways. They turned aside after dishonest gain and accepted bribes and perverted justice.
>
> So all the elders of Israel gathered together and came to Samuel at Ramah. They said to him, "You are old, and your sons do not follow your ways; now appoint a king to lead us, such as all the other nations have."
>
> But when they said, "Give us a king to lead us," this displeased Samuel; so he prayed to the LORD. And the LORD told him: "Listen to all that the people are saying to you; it is not you they have rejected, but they have rejected me as their king. As they have done from the day I brought them up out of Egypt until this day, forsaking me and serving other gods, so they are doing to you."

Samuel was a prophet and judge for the people of Israel. As you can see in this passage, he had an intimate relationship with God. This close relationship began in his childhood, which is a fascinating story told in 1 Samuel 1–3.

As Samuel was aging, he wanted to facilitate a leadership transition to his sons. The problem was that his sons were not enough like him, and the people rejected that idea. It was at that point that they posed their own solution, the idea of having a king. Notice the people's reasoning for the request: it was simply because they wanted to be like everyone else.

Is that such a bad idea? we ask. Surely it is a reasonable option to consider. What is such a big deal about wanting to be like everyone else? To understand this you have to look back at Exodus 19:1–8.

> On the first day of the third month after the Israelites left Egypt—on the very day—they came to the Desert of Sinai. After they set out from Rephidim, they entered the Desert of Sinai, and Israel camped there in the desert in front of the mountain.
>
> Then Moses went up to God, and the LORD called to him from the mountain and said, "This is what you are to say to the house of Jacob and what you are to tell the people of Israel: 'You yourselves have seen what I did to Egypt, and how I carried you on eagles' wings and brought you to myself. Now if you obey me fully and keep my covenant, then out of all nations you will be my treasured possession. Although the whole earth is mine, you will be for me a kingdom of priests and a holy nation.' These are the words you are to speak to the Israelites."
>
> So Moses went back and summoned the elders of the people and set before them all the words the LORD had commanded him to speak. The people all responded together, "We will do everything the LORD has said." So Moses brought their answer back to the LORD.

Israel had never had a human king since its beginning as a nation, and God never intended for them to have one. God had called Israel to be different. He had offered them a special place in history. He wanted them to be his people, his unique kingdom. He had demonstrated what this could look like through rescuing them from Egypt. It was not that his people would not go through experiences like the trials of living in Egypt, but he promised to care for them in those trials. The picture of the kind of care he wanted to lavish on them is beautiful: "I carried you on eagles' wings and brought you to myself."

God explained that this was not because he loved the children of Israel more than others, but because he had a special role for them. He wanted to be their king. He wanted to model something different with them. He wanted the rest of the earth to understand what it looks like to belong to him and to be his people because that is his goal for all the people of the earth.

Since creation all God has wanted is to love the children he created and have them love him in return. The children of Israel were set apart to model this. God explained that purpose to Abraham in Genesis 12.

> The LORD had said to Abram, "Leave your country, your people and your father's household and go to the land I will show you.
>
> > "I will make you into a great nation,
> >
> > > and I will bless you;
> >
> > I will make your name great,
> >
> > > and you will be a blessing.
> >
> > I will bless those who bless you,
> >
> > > and whoever curses you I will curse;
> >
> > and all peoples on earth
> >
> > > will be blessed through you." (vv. 1–3)

As God explained it here to Abram, he intended for his people to be a blessing to the whole earth. That was the calling of Israel, and of course that calling has transferred to us today as believers who make up his bride, the church. That was the result of Christ's death and resurrection.

Today when we in any way reject God as king in our lives, we repeat the tragedy of 1 Samuel 8. We tell God it is nice to have him around, but what we would really like is to take our destiny into our own hands. We want to look like everyone else and not be those who are called out to be different, a people set apart for God's purposes. Often we do this daily through our actions, if not through our words.

Samuel Had an Intimate Relationship with God

The second foundational piece we need to understand about the background of the stories of Saul and David is getting to know Samuel. To look at the life of Samuel is to see one very clear picture of what it means to be a leader after God's heart.

Samuel, like all the Christlike leaders throughout the Bible, walked closely with God. He listened to God's voice and obeyed whatever God asked, no matter what the cost to him personally. Unlike some of the other biblical examples we have been given, Samuel was completely single minded in this role and never wavered from it, from childhood to death, as far as we know.

When you read the first few chapters of 1 Samuel, you get some of the details of Samuel's life and leadership. You find that Samuel was dedicated to God by his mother, Hannah, before he was ever conceived. Samuel literally grew up in the temple, learning from an early age to expect to hear God's voice and obey it. You find that Samuel was God's mouthpiece to his people over and over again. You see times when the people of Israel turned back to God because they listened to Samuel and obeyed his words. You also see God blessing Israel as a result. You can see that God defeated their enemies, the Philistines, throughout Samuel's reign.

It was not that Samuel lived some kind of charmed life, however. He had to fight many battles, and he certainly felt the same pain that all leaders feel. He fought the Philistines regularly. When the people rejected Samuel's choice of his sons to be their leaders, as we read in this story, he was deeply saddened. Later when Saul failed so miserably in his role of king, Samuel was depressed. He felt the agonizing pain that God feels when his people reject him.

It is instructive to see Samuel's reaction to the difficulties that confronted him. He always went to God, unburdened himself to the One he trusted completely, and received God's consolation. Then in dialogue with God, he received his instructions and thoroughly carried them out.

The record of Samuel's conversations with God is marvelous and rich in detail. From the time of his childhood until the time of his death, Samuel's interactions with God focused on providing leadership for God's people and obedience to God's will. This lovely relationship between Samuel and God is one of the most gripping tales of intimacy you will find in Scripture.

God Called, Anointed, and Empowered Both Saul and David

Now we move to a third important piece of background in these events, and this one I find deeply disturbing. When comparing the stories of Saul and David, there are many similarities, especially in their beginnings. And this list of similarities may challenge many of our traditions and even our theology when we consider them carefully. Both Saul and David were chosen by God to be the king. They were both handpicked by Samuel out of the entire nation. They were both anointed by him with oil. Then the accounts clearly state they were both filled with God's Spirit and had their hearts changed.

Most of us hold certain firm ideas about God's calling on the lives of his leaders. Interestingly those firm ideas vary depending on what denominational tradition we come from. We often give tremendous weight to whether or not a leader is "called" and how that calling occurred.

In some traditions we use the laying on of hands to confirm a calling and to confer position or ordination. In some we anoint the appointee with oil and pray over that person. In others it is a group of elders or the outgoing leader who confers positional authority to an incoming leader, often through some gesture that usually includes praying over that person.

Most Christian leaders draw their strength and their validity from a sense of their calling and being chosen by God for a certain job. They believe that their authority to lead is given to them by the process through which they come into leadership. Even in a completely secular position we are most comfortable when we are hired for a job because those hiring us believe we are well qualified and will do well. If you are an incoming executive officer, you know, for example, that you need the approval of the board.

So while we could argue about which method of confirming the calling of a leader is most correct, we can easily agree that every leader needs to know that the ones putting them in the position believe it is right and that they are qualified.

What is startling in these stories of Saul and David is how similar are their beginnings. Let's look at the descriptions of the calling of both Saul and David and ask God to give us insight. We will start with Saul in 1 Samuel 9:

> Now the day before Saul came, the LORD had revealed this to Samuel: "About this time tomorrow I will send you a man from the land of Benjamin. Anoint him ruler over my people Israel; he will deliver them from the hand of the Philistines. I have looked on my people, for their cry has reached me."
>
> When Samuel caught sight of Saul, the LORD said to him, "This is the man I spoke to you about; he will govern my people."
>
> . . . After they came down from the high place to the town, Samuel talked with Saul on the roof of his house. They rose about daybreak, and Samuel called to Saul on the roof, "Get ready, and I will send you on your way." When Saul got ready, he and Samuel went outside together. As they were going down to the edge

of the town, Samuel said to Saul, "Tell the servant to go on ahead of us"—and the servant did so—"but you stay here for a while, so that I may give you a message from God."

Then Samuel took a bottle of olive oil and poured it on Saul's head and kissed him, saying, "Has not the LORD anointed you ruler over his inheritance?" (1 Samuel 9:15–10:1)

Saul and one of his father's servants had been sent on a journey to search for lost donkeys. We do not get the feeling that this was a particularly exciting job, and they were certainly not very successful in the undertaking. They had nearly given up when the servant remembers that there is a prophet in the next town and suggests that they could ask him for help.

This is how they encounter Samuel. They seek his help in finding the lost donkeys. What Saul is *not* seeking is an appointment as king. If you read all the verses, you find that he protests to Samuel that he is the least of the least and is confused as to why Samuel would single him out. Later at the first public announcement of his kingship, he hides! This is further proof that being king is not a role he is seeking or thinks he is worthy of.

It seems that God understood Saul's personality, or at least his reluctance, because he has Samuel go into detail with Saul about the things that will happen after he anoints Saul. This is probably to reassure him about the validity of Samuel's words. Let's look at what Samuel says to Saul.

"When you leave me today, you will meet two men near Rachel's tomb, at Zelzah on the border of Benjamin. They will say to you, 'The donkeys you set out to look for have been found. And now your father has stopped thinking about them and is worried about you. He is asking, "What shall I do about my son?"'

"Then you will go on from there until you reach

the great tree of Tabor. Three men going up to God at Bethel will meet you there. One will be carrying three young goats, another three loaves of bread, and another a skin of wine. They will greet you and offer you two loaves of bread, which you will accept from them.

"After that you will go to Gibeah of God, where there is a Philistine outpost. As you approach the town, you will meet a procession of prophets coming down from the high place with lyres, timbrels, pipes and harps being played before them, and they will be prophesying. The Spirit of the LORD will come on you in power, and you will prophesy with them; and you will be changed into a different person. Once these signs are fulfilled, do whatever your hand finds to do, for God is with you.

"Go down ahead of me to Gilgal. I will surely come down to you to sacrifice burnt offerings and fellowship offerings, but you must wait seven days until I come to you and tell you what you are to do."

As Saul turned to leave Samuel, God changed Saul's heart, and all these signs were fulfilled that day. (1 Samuel 10:2–9)

Then the Bible goes into great detail to repeat exactly what happened as Saul left, showing that it all took place just as Samuel said it would. God seems to want to give Saul plenty of evidence that this calling is supernatural, that it is from God, and that Samuel is truly appointed to anoint him.

A few verses later we see the way Samuel announces Saul's appointment to the people of Israel. He doesn't ask them to assume he has heard from God. Instead the people go through a process of "casting lots"—sort like throwing dice—to reveal whom God has chosen, and this process points to Saul. Casting lots was a culturally acceptable method of confirming God's message to his people. It is encouraging how flexible God is in confirming his word to us. He will go to great lengths to work within our local cultural context to share with us his will.

First through speaking to Samuel and then through the casting of lots, God makes his choice unmistakable to his people. He has chosen Saul. Samuel anoints him with oil as a symbol of placing God's anointing on him.

Now let us compare Saul's appointment with David's appointment. We find this story in 1 Samuel 16.

> The LORD said to Samuel, "How long will you mourn for Saul, since I have rejected him as king over Israel? Fill your horn with oil and be on your way; I am sending you to Jesse of Bethlehem. I have chosen one of his sons to be king."
>
> . . . When they arrived, Samuel saw Eliab and thought, "Surely the LORD's anointed stands here before the LORD."
>
> But the LORD said to Samuel, "Do not consider his appearance or his height, for I have rejected him. The LORD does not look at the things human beings look at. People look at the outward appearance, but the LORD looks at the heart."
>
> Then Jesse called Abinadab and had him pass in front of Samuel. But Samuel said, "The LORD has not chosen this one either." Jesse then had Shammah pass by, but Samuel said, "Nor has the LORD chosen this one." Jesse had seven of his sons pass before Samuel, but Samuel said to him, "The LORD has not chosen these." So he asked Jesse, "Are these all the sons you have?"
>
> "There is still the youngest," Jesse answered. "He is tending the sheep." Samuel said, "Send for him; we will not sit down until he arrives."
>
> So he sent and had him brought in. He was glowing

with health and had a fine appearance and handsome features.

Then the LORD said, "Rise and anoint him; this is the one."

So Samuel took the horn of oil and anointed him in the presence of his brothers, and from that day on the Spirit of the LORD came on David in power. Samuel then went to Ramah. (1 Samuel 16:1–13)

While a few of the details are different, essentially the same process takes place. Because God has rejected Saul as king, he tells Samuel to anoint someone else as king. At the risk of his own life, Samuel obeys.

God tells Samuel that he is to anoint one of Jesse's sons. Samuel initially does not know which son, but he does exactly what God tells him and goes to Jesse's house. As one son after another comes to meet Samuel, Samuel listens to hear from God if this is the one. When it seems that Jesse is about to run out of sons, he calls the very youngest one from the fields; and as David arrives, God tells Samuel that this is the one.

Samuel publicly anoints David in front of his entire family. David is neither looking for such a role nor expecting it. He is merely a shepherd boy, who no one expects much from. Similar to Saul, David is just as surprised as anyone else that Samuel has chosen him.

Even more chilling in some ways is the description of what happens after Samuel anoints both Saul and David. Let's look at the verses.

As Saul turned to leave Samuel, God changed Saul's heart, and all these signs were fulfilled that day. (1 Samuel 10:9)

So Samuel took the horn of oil and anointed him in the presence of his brothers, and from that day on the

Spirit of the LORD came on David in power. Samuel then went to Ramah. (1 Samuel 16:13)

In each case God does something amazing, unique, and pivotal in each boy as soon as Samuel anoints him. In the case of Saul, it says that God "changed" Saul's heart. In the case of David, we see that the Spirit of the Lord came on David in power.

While it would be nice to try to start drawing a distinction at this point between the two stories, the reality is that the similarities far outweigh any differences. Each was clearly chosen by God for the role of king, and neither was looking for the job. In fact, each was quite young, still living at home and working for his father, and unmarried. You get the feeling that neither they nor anyone around them thought they were an obvious choice for the role.

They each signal acceptance of what Samuel is saying to them in some way, or at least we know that they allow Samuel to anoint each of them with oil, which Samuel does in obedience to God's instruction. And then most disturbing of all in many ways, it is abundantly clear that God supernaturally and spiritually equips each for the task.

Let's Look at the End of Their Stories

Let's look at how these stories end to appreciate how chilling it is that their beginnings were so similar.

Saul reigned for forty-two years, and his reign ended after he suffered critical wounds in battle and then killed himself rather than let the enemy capture him. Much earlier in Saul's reign God's Spirit left him, and God told Samuel, "I regret that I have made Saul king, because he has turned away from me and has not carried out my instructions" (1 Samuel 15:11).

David also reigned about the same length of time, forty years, but David's life ended peacefully when he died of old age. God's description of David comes in many different passages, and one of the most telling is that God called David "a man after his own heart" (1 Samuel 13:14). God promised to establish David's kingdom forever because of God's great love for David.

As we study these two stories more deeply, we will see over and over that Saul's leadership causes God deep grief, while David's leadership brought God abundant joy. There could not be a starker difference in their outcomes from God's perspective.

When we read the end of their stories, we want to find something at the beginning that foreshadows their very different ends, but in reality it is not there. We want to deny that Saul was God's chosen or that he was anointed and filled with God's Spirit. We want to believe that somehow David was special to God from the beginning but that Saul was not.

We not only want to believe this, but also need to believe it, because if that is not the case, then the terrible ending of Saul's reign seems nearly impossible to understand. We do not want it to be possible for God's chosen, anointed, and Spirit-filled leader to be able to fail so miserably. It is frightening, terrifying in fact, because ultimately it means that this could happen to any one of us.

This is what compels us to ask the rest of the questions in this book. This is what forces us to deeply search our own lives and leadership. This is what puts us on our knees before the God of the universe, asking him in humility to search our hearts and heal them.

Now let me encourage you that before you go any further, please stop and pray. Do not bother to read the rest of this book unless you are willing to allow the incredible searchlight of the Holy Spirit to have full freedom to shine brightly on every hidden detail of your life and leadership. All God wants to do is love us, heal us, and draw us closer.

So beware: God could use this process to help you grow. That is the challenge before you. Are you willing to honestly answer the questions that follow? Are you willing to seriously search and discover if your leadership looks more like Saul's or David's? Are you willing to let God deal honestly with what you discover?

Questions for Reflection:

- What do you find most surprising about the similarities between the story of Saul and the story of David?
- Have you ever known a leader who was godly and wise for a number of years and then departed from God's ways? As you recall that story, what do you believe happened in that leader's life?
- Do you believe this happens often? Explain your answer.

QUESTION 1:
Do I Fear People More Than God?

I was sitting in a beautiful old Methodist church in northern India one day, listening as some of our Development Associates International (DAI) staff conducted a workshop on the concept of servant leadership with a number of local Christian leaders. I happened to be sitting by the bishop of the region, an apparently wonderful Christian leader who had intentionally chosen to take time out of his busy schedule to participate with his leaders in this workshop.

We were using our core case study about a Christian leader, Reverend Ogulu, in the fictional country of Kabuli, who regularly uses his position of power for his own benefit. The case study describes how Reverend Ogulu gets the biggest office, the chauffeured car, all the other perks of the office, and plenty of speaking engagements overseas that he uses to benefit himself or family members. It also explains that his office is always a hive of activity, with people coming and going because they are seeking his approval out of fear of doing anything of substance without his blessing.

The case study states that Reverend Ogulu started out with the best of intentions, a pure heart and zeal for the mission. But over time, and especially after experiencing some betrayal by a staff member, his role has evolved into one of dictatorial command. He alone controls all of the resources and never utilizes the expertise of his staff. He has no real accountability except to God alone.

As the story became even more descriptive, the bishop leaned over to me with a naughty grin on his face. "You know, you didn't have to use a made-up country like Kabuli. You could have just said, 'India,' because everything you are describing is just exactly the way we top leaders behave here!"

"Absolute Power Corrupts Absolutely"

There is really nothing new under the sun, is there? If you know the story of Saul, you see it repeated daily throughout the world. A humble, good leader who is filled with God's Spirit gets put in a powerful leadership role—leadership always carries power.

Slowly, over time that power becomes more important to him than he ever thought possible, and he finds himself doing whatever it takes to stay in power. And rather than using that power for the good of others, he begins to use it for himself. As Lord Acton's famous dictum says, "Power tends to corrupt, and absolute power corrupts absolutely."

Saul, the first earthly king of Israel, fell into this trap. Although he started out so humbled by the idea of being king that he hid when Samuel wanted to announce his kingship, he soon reveled in the power of the role. When David appeared on the scene, killed Goliath, and began being successful in every battle, Saul became jealous.

I am reminded of a conversation I had with a leader from Ethiopia. It came as a great revelation to me as I was beginning to work in the area of leadership development years ago. The conversation began with me explaining to him some of DAI's programs that were designed specifically to help older leaders mentor younger ones.

"Oh, Jane," he said, "let me explain to you what happens when we older leaders see a younger leader with lots of potential coming up. Do you know what we do?"

"No," I shook my head, "what do you do?" I waited with great anticipation. I was fully expecting to learn about wonderful local church practices of leadership development that might be useful in another location.

"We smash them!" came his response. And to demonstrate, he lifted his foot and hurled it to the ground, twisting it left and right as if squishing a bug under his shoe. "We are afraid the younger leader will come up and take our job, so we make sure that he's stopped before he ever gets started!"

Even though he said this with a gleam in his eye, nothing had prepared me for that honest and chilling answer. How could it be that older Christian leaders would intentionally seek to destroy younger leaders because they feared they would take their jobs?

In 1 Samuel 18:7 the Bible says that as Saul and David returned from battle the women of Israel came out to meet Saul with dancing and joyful songs that included "Saul has slain his thousands, and David his tens of thousands."

And what was Saul's response in his heart of hearts? "Saul was very angry; this refrain displeased him greatly. 'They have credited David with tens of thousands,' he thought, 'but me with only thousands. What more can he get but the kingdom?'" (v. 8).

From there Saul spiraled lower and lower as he tried to destroy David through setting him up to be killed by the Philistines and eventually trying to personally hunt him down and kill him.

How did Saul go from being God's anointed leader to being someone trying to kill God's anointed leader? It is an interesting progression and a frightening one if you have ever held a role of leadership, because Saul began with innocence and humility.

How Did Saul Respond under Pressure?

Leadership always brings pressure. Always. While leadership often looks like an attractive role from the outside, one of the painful realities is that it carries with it unexpected challenges. There will always be things going on that destroy your plans or call for resources or answers you do not have.

In political and business leadership this happens all of the time. President George W. Bush would never have predicted that the terrorist attacks of September 11, 2001, would completely overshadow his plans for his presidency. European airline industry leaders would hardly have guessed that a volcano in Iceland would cost their companies millions of euros. The financial recession beginning in 2008 caused powerful businesses to fail. As a result, some of the most secure bankers and Wall Street executives found themselves without jobs overnight. Everything they were building, dreaming about, and planning vanished before their eyes.

Saul had an incredibly difficult challenge of this type early in his leadership. When he first became king, he had the confidence of the people as he won a great battle. Just as he was riding the crest of success from that battle, the Philistines took offense because Jonathan attacked a Philistine outpost. So they gathered their forces together to teach the Israelites a lesson.

The description of the Philistine army that gathered is impressive: "The Philistines assembled to fight Israel, with three thousand chariots, six thousand charioteers, and soldiers as numerous as the sand on the seashore" (1 Samuel 13:5).

Then we see the response by Israel's army to this sea of Philistine soldiers: "When the Israelites saw that their situation was critical and that their army was hard pressed, they hid in caves and thickets, among the rocks, and in pits and cisterns. Some Hebrews even crossed the Jordan to the land of Gad and Gilead. Saul remained at Gilgal, and all the troops with him were quaking with fear" (1 Samuel 13:6–7).

Later in the chapter we find that this was not just idle fear. Apparently the Philistines had a monopoly on blacksmithing and therefore the Israelites had no weapons—absolutely none, except Jonathan and Saul each had one sword. Here they were facing a fully armed force complete with chariots, and they had nothing but their bare hands to fight with.

The situation was dire. Saul was the king, and everyone was looking to him for answers. He knew that the next critical step was to offer sacrifices to God. The pressure was mounting, and after waiting what must have seemed like an eternity he made a decision to take things into his own hands.

> He waited seven days, the time set by Samuel; but Samuel did not come to Gilgal, and Saul's men began to scatter. So he said, "Bring me the burnt offering and the fellowship offerings." And Saul offered up the burnt offering. Just as he finished making the offering, Samuel arrived, and Saul went out to greet him.
>
> "What have you done?" asked Samuel.
>
> Saul replied, "When I saw that the men were scattering, and that you did not come at the set time, and that the Philistines were assembling at Mikmash, I thought, 'Now the Philistines will come down against me at Gilgal, and I have not sought the LORD's favor.' So I felt compelled to offer the burnt offering."
>
> "You have done a foolish thing," Samuel said. "You have not kept the command the LORD your God gave you; if you had, he would have established your kingdom over Israel for all time. But now your kingdom will not endure; the LORD has sought out a man after his own heart and appointed him ruler of his people, because you have not kept the LORD's command." (1 Samuel 13:8–14)

Saul's decision was understandable, it was logical, and it was easily justified; but it was horribly wrong. Can you feel the tremendous pressure in that one statement from Saul in verse 11—"When I saw that the men were scattering"? Have you ever been in that position where followers are leaving you because you are doing the right thing instead of what they thought you should be doing?

Instead of following Samuel's orders from God and obeying and trusting God for the outcomes despite how things looked, Saul caved into the pressure and took things into his own hands. He didn't do some horrible thing, like make a sacrifice to other gods. He did the right thing but did it the wrong way.

This is clearly a heart issue. This is about trusting God, despite how things appear. This is a regular, sometimes daily choice in leadership. Do I fear people more than I fear God? Whom do I trust more, God or myself? And this is the pivotal point where so many leaders fail today as well.

I was meeting with a group of leaders in India a few years ago. They were business executives and heads of large ministries and denominations. We were talking about biblical servant leadership and how radical it would be if practiced in their settings. Their response was surprising, but understandable. "We cannot practice this type of leadership," they said uniformly, "because it is not what people expect from a leader in this culture. We wish we could, but it is impossible. We have to be the big boss and be demanding. If we don't, our people will not respect us!"

Just recently I heard the same sentiment repeated in Russia from a church bishop there. His comment continues to echo in my mind: "Of course I understand what servant leadership is. I preach on it regularly. But I cannot practice it because it could never work here. You see, this is Russia!"

What kind of excuses do we make for failing to do what God has commanded? How often do we take things in our own hands and decide what is right and wrong for us, despite what we know are God's will and his ways? How many times do we simply do what we think will work because we believe that to do otherwise might threaten our position or our reputation?

How Did David Respond under Pressure?

David faced military battles regularly throughout his leadership of Israel as well. In fact, it was usually the aggressive Philistines who had to be confronted, just as in Saul's case. Over and over the Philistines challenged Israel. While many of us today do not face military battles as our leadership challenges, it is not so hard to imagine the type of pressure David faced as we read the biblical accounts.

David had just become king over Israel in chapter 5 of 2 Samuel when the Philistines came after him. This first half of chapter 5 is all about David's victories, about how God is honoring him and making it abundantly clear that he is God's man for this position. The chapter is all about David becoming king over all of Israel, of his kingdom being established, and of him becoming more and more powerful.

Let's pick up the story from verse 17: "When the Philistines heard that David had been anointed king over Israel, they went up in full force to search for him, but David heard about it and went down to the stronghold. Now the Philistines had come and spread out in the Valley of Rephaim; so David inquired of the LORD, 'Shall I go and attack the Philistines? Will you deliver them into my hands?'"

This is an interesting and very humble stance that David took at this point. Remember this is a time of great excitement of finally coming into the role of king God had promised him years before. So this was very similar timing in David's kingship as the challenge to Saul in our earlier passage. For both of these kings, the stories we are comparing here took place not long after they became king and while they were still relishing the power and honor of the role.

David had been a warrior and a commander of troops for some time. This was not his first confrontation with the Philistines. It was not as if he had no idea of how to respond to them, and he had many troops at his command. Yet he had developed a habit of always asking God what to do. And God responded very specifically.

Let's continue in verses 19–21: "The LORD answered him, 'Go, for I will surely deliver the Philistines into your hands.' So David went to Baal Perazim, and there he defeated them. He said, 'As waters break out, the LORD has broken out against my enemies before me.' So that place was called Baal Perazim. The Philistines abandoned their idols there, and David and his men carried them off."

Wouldn't it be wonderful if as leaders we had to fight the battles only once, if our enemies would accept defeat and leave us alone! David's experience confirms for us that in this world that is rarely the case.

> Once more the Philistines came up and spread out in the Valley of Rephaim; so David inquired of the LORD, and he answered, "Do not go straight up, but circle around behind them and attack them in front of the poplar trees. As soon as you hear the sound of marching in the tops of the poplar trees, move quickly, because that will mean the LORD has gone out in front of you to strike the Philistine army." So David did as the LORD commanded him, and he struck down the Philistines all the way from Gibeon to Gezer. (vv. 22–25)

I find this passage especially moving as I read it through. Think about the context. The Philistines have come to fight David, and the first time he inquired of the Lord what to do. God answered him and David obeyed and they were defeated.

The situation repeated itself and rather than presume in pride that he knew what to do, David again inquired of the Lord. What amazing humility! And interestingly enough God gave different instructions the second time. He told David not to go straight up, but to circle around behind them. In this case God had gone out in front of David to strike down the Philistine army.

They fought the battle together, David and God. God did his part and invited David to join in at a certain point. This is so typical of God's ways, but we miss this regularly. So often we are called by God to take on a task, a mission, or a pastorate, to play a political leadership role, or to run a business. We usually begin by getting some training and slowly start to grow in experience.

When things begin to go really well, we often get comfortable with our own expertise. We say through our actions, "Thanks, God; I've got it from here. I'll check back with you if there is a crisis; but, other than that, I'd like to get on with this on my own now."

Then we are shocked that God is disappointed in us, that he withdraws and lets us do it on our own, and that he seems far off when that crisis comes, or the financial disaster, or whatever it is that wakes us from our prideful stupor.

We so often miss the whole point. God isn't all that interested in us accomplishing a task. Isn't it obvious that he could do everything in this world that he wants to on his own, if he chose to do so? He is pleased with our successes and wants us to do his work, but primarily what he is after is relationship with us.

I often think that our work must look to God like the art that young children bring home to us from kindergarten. They are so proud of their crayon drawings, and of course we are as well. When we hang a drawing on the refrigerator, it is not because we have no prettier picture to grace that space. We hang it there because we love that child so much, and we love the fact that our child brought it home as a gift to us.

I will never forget how this lesson became real to me while attending a wonderful church service in the United States at Christmas one year. The church had an outreach for those with mental disabilities. Every Christmas they brought the whole Sunday school class of mentally disabled people to the front of the church to perform a special song they had prepared.

Even the process of getting the whole group to the front of the church took a long time, as some were physically challenged as well. Corralling them and getting them to stand facing the right direction was even a bit of a battle. Their musical performance was definitely something to behold, since they rarely were on the same verse of the song, let alone on the same tune. Yet their beaming smiles at the congregation's standing ovation made the whole event so worthwhile for everyone involved. As the pastor later pointed out, our most accomplished musicians probably sound like that to God, in comparison with the angels' songs. Yet our Father loves it when we sing songs of worship.

God wants us to do exactly what David did—ask him at every juncture what to do. He wants to be walking with us, talking with us daily, hourly, moment by moment, so that the most natural thing in the world is to ask him what to do in every situation.

For David, there was still a battle to fight. It was dirty work, frightening, and hard. God didn't do all the work, and he didn't solve all of the problems. He left David to do his part. That points out the other mistake we often make: we think that if God is with us there will be no battles. Everything will be fine, and there will be no dirty jobs. But that is also not the case.

God does not do everything for us. He leaves us part of the task to complete. I believe this is because he wants us in something like an apprenticeship. We work with him, learning his ways in the heat of the battle and the pressures of life, so that we grow in godliness and character.

This is all part of spiritual maturity. We naturally want everything to be simple and smooth. We scream in protest when things do not go the way we planned and we don't get what we want. Meanwhile God uses the brokenness and pain of this world to help us learn to trust him and walk in his ways. He does not promise everything will be perfect, but he does promise he will never leave us to walk through the pain alone.

One of the most fascinating leaders I have ever met is a Ugandan man who loves Jesus. He was a young man and a believer when Idi Amin came to power. Amin was the ruthless dictator who nearly destroyed Uganda with his bizarre behavior and merciless killings. This young man was appointed by Amin to head the government unit that was designed to stamp out all illegal worship in the country. This included the house churches in which this young man worshiped.

Throughout the years of Amin's reign this man lived a double life at the request of the church leaders. He would go to his government office every day and plot strategies to destroy the church. Then as he sent officers out the front door to attack a house church meeting, he would send colleagues out the back door with the urgent message to warn the believers before the government officials could get there. Sometimes the informants got there before the police, and sometimes they didn't.

Everyone felt that with him inside the government they had a better chance of surviving. It must have been unbelievable pressure to live through. Yet he daily did his best to protect every believer he could. And strangely enough, Amin never suspected him of leading a double life. God protected him throughout those years of agony.

I never heard him ask why. Why didn't God stop Amin sooner, rather than let him kill untold numbers of Christians and other innocent people and nearly destroy an entire nation? Instead his faith is deep and solid and sweet. He is a man who learned to fear God more than evil people and to trust God more than himself.

Though that is an amazing and sensational example of trusting God, I believe that the daily challenges many of us face in our leadership are just as telling. Aren't we constantly tempted to take things into our own hands and abandon God's ways because "we know his ways won't work"? How many of us have failed to tithe on our income or to give generously to a cause when God prompted us because "we just don't have the money right now"?

What about the opportunities to stop and encourage a friend or listen to a needy neighbor, which we fail to do because "we are too busy with our ministry"? Are God's ways really so impractical? Have we become so saturated with our culture that we have no idea what the culture of the kingdom of God looks like and asks of us?

I think that too often we don't really believe what God says. We do not believe we can trust him. We think we know better, so we take matters into our own hands.

Saul and David were each confronted with the Philistine army and a hopeless battle to fight. Saul chose to trust his own judgment when the pressure mounted. In that process he disobeyed God in such a serious way that God's response was to remove the kingdom from him.

David, on the other hand, chose to ask God what to do, not once but every time he confronted a challenge, even if it was the same challenge as before. David refused to even engage in the battle until he heard clearly from God. Then when he did hear, he obediently cooperated with God's strategy, even though it wasn't totally rational from a human viewpoint. The result was victory for God's people.

God chose both Saul and David for leadership and equipped them for their tasks. But each man made very different choices of who to trust when faced with the pressures of leadership. Which one do you most closely resemble? Does your leadership look more like Saul's or David's?

Questions for Reflection:

- Have you ever trusted in your own logic rather than waiting for God to act? Give an example.
- Has fear of losing your title and position ever led you to do the wrong thing? Give an example.
- Have you ever presumed that because God once said to do a task a certain way that you should just keep doing it that way?

QUESTION 2:
Do I Use Up or Build Up People under My Leadership?

I recently heard the testimony of an older Christian Indian leader who had just finished a leadership development course related to the management of people. In his testimony he said that his life and leadership had been turned upside down by the course and its implications.

He shared that he had been very "successful" at whatever he undertook because he knew how to make people do what he wanted. He had often been promoted because of his effectiveness. He was a senior executive, an administrator, with the reputation of getting things done and getting them done right.

He had always viewed those who worked for him as tools to get the task done. Now after taking the course, he was looking back and realizing that what he had been doing was using people and sometimes abusing them. He didn't care how many hours they worked, whether they received the training they needed, or whether they had benefits. It just wasn't his problem.

He said he knew that what he was doing was wrong. But he always justified his mistreatment of others by saying to himself that he was only doing what was necessary to produce a good product.

How many Christian leaders do you know who would fit the description of "people users"? Have you ever worked for one of them? What was that like?

What Was It like to Work for Saul?

Let's turn once again to Saul and David to see what we can learn on this subject of how we treat those who work under us. We find an interesting story in 1 Samuel 14. We pick up the story where we left off with Saul and the army of Israel facing an enormous Philistine force. The Israelites were outnumbered and "outgunned," as it were, because the Israelites had no weapons except for those of Saul and his son Jonathan.

Without telling anyone, Jonathan and his armor-bearer took an enormous step of faith and decided to attack a small Philistine outpost. They decided to test whether God wanted them to make the attack by letting the soldiers see them at the bottom of the cliff. If the Philistine soldiers invited them up to fight, they believed it was God's sign that he was going to give them the battle. And, indeed, Jonathan and his armor-bearer were invited to the outpost, and they defeated the Philistines there, killing twenty in all.

Not only do they win a victory, but God blessed and multiplied their efforts and willingness to take the risk by bringing a panic on the Philistine army. The confusion was so great that several verses later, when Saul and the rest of the army finally joined the battle, the Philistines began killing each other.

The leadership problem of using people rather than empowering them surfaces as the Israelites pursued their enemies into the woods to kill them: "Now the Israelites were in distress that day, because Saul had bound the people under an oath, saying, 'Cursed be anyone who eats food before evening comes, before I have avenged myself on my enemies!' So none of the troops tasted food" (v. 24).

So the situation we have here is the whole army under pressure and pursuing the enemy, but Saul had forced them to fast. This was not a call to fast in order to seek God's favor, but instead it was apparently an issue of pride for Saul. He focused attention on himself and his status rather than on the needs of his troops and on God's provision.

Interestingly the passage tells us that when the troops entered the woods, there was honey everywhere. God had provided for his people, and yet none of the soldiers except Jonathan ate the honey. Jonathan was not around when his father swore the oath, so he didn't know anything about it. Innocently he ate and regained needed strength. Then he was surprised that no one else ate. That was when they told him about Saul's oath. His response is instructive: "Jonathan said, 'My father has made trouble for the country. See how my eyes brightened when I tasted a little of this honey. How much better it would have been if the men had eaten today some of the plunder they took from their enemies. Would not the slaughter of the Philistines have been even greater?'" (vv. 29–30).

Why did Saul issue this decree about the army not being allowed to eat on the day of battle? It is hard to tell exactly, but what seems to be clear is that it was more about Saul's ego than about anything else. It does not seem to have had anything to do with God's glory, and it was not in the best interests of the fighting men. They are described as being "in distress" so obviously they were physically suffering.

The troops were so hungry that when evening came and they were released from Saul's oath, they ate the plunder in ways that contravened the laws of God. So Saul through his selfish actions actually provoked his men to sin.

Jonathan's response confirms that. After he accidentally broke his father's decree and then learned about this oath, he expressed his opinion of how foolish and cruel it was.

How many times do we as leaders take on a task or agree to implement a new program without thinking about the implications for our staff. Do we ever do it because we know it will add to our reputation, without considering the burden it will put on others? Do we do it for the sake of our pride? Do we justify our mistreatment of others by saying it is "for the sake of the kingdom of God"?

I will never forget my husband coming home from a meeting of the ministry he was working for at the time, bewildered by what he had heard at that evening's meeting. The founder of the mission had gotten up to share with great excitement a vision he had for bringing the gospel to the unreached. The vision had to do with carrying out a global activity that was extremely complex to execute.

Immediately my husband, who is an administrative genius, began thinking about what it would require to implement this plan. He and many others in the audience lost their enthusiasm quickly for the vision because they knew from past experience that they would have to be the ones to turn this vision into reality. They were overwhelmed with the thought of what this would cost in terms of time, money, and effort.

Obviously the visionary leader had never counted the cost when he had decided to undertake this idea. Even as he shared it passionately, it was clear that it never occurred to him that his bright idea could cost some of his staff years of their lives and ministries.

Now we come to one of the more revealing parts of Saul's story:

> Saul said, "Let us go down and pursue the Philistines by night and plunder them till dawn, and let us not leave one of them alive."
>
> "Do whatever seems best to you," they replied.
> But the priest said, "Let us inquire of God here."
> So Saul asked God, "Shall I go down and pursue

the Philistines? Will you give them into Israel's hand?" But God did not answer him that day.

Saul therefore said, "Come here, all you who are leaders of the army, and let us find out what sin has been committed today." (1 Samuel 14:36–38)

Saul was so excited about the victory they were experiencing that he wanted to pursue the army of the Philistines, and the soldiers agreed. But the priest spoke up and reminded Saul that they should inquire of the Lord, and Saul complied. And when God failed to respond, Saul understood that he must do something to find out why God was not responding.

This segment of the story reveals a "lukewarmness" toward God that I find particularly disturbing. Saul was not against God. He understood that he was to follow his ways and complied with that idea when reminded. In the excitement of the moment, he just didn't think about asking for God's guidance. God's perspective was not a high priority in Saul's mind.

Saul did know that God's failure to respond to the priest's inquiry meant that something was not right. He had an understanding of that. Yet for him it was an afterthought.

At this point in the story Saul figured out through their cultural system of casting lots who disobeyed his decree.

Saul therefore said, "Come here, all you who are leaders of the army, and let us find out what sin has been committed today. As surely as the LORD who rescues Israel lives, even if it lies with my son Jonathan, he must die." But not one of them said a word.

Saul then said to all the Israelites, "You stand over there; I and Jonathan my son will stand over here."

"Do what seems best to you," they replied.

Then Saul prayed to the LORD, the God of Israel, "Why have you not answered your servant today? If the fault is in me or my son Jonathan, respond with

Urim, but if the men of Israel are at fault, respond with Thummim." Jonathan and Saul were taken by lot, and the men were cleared. Saul said, "Cast the lot between me and Jonathan my son." And Jonathan was taken.

Then Saul said to Jonathan, "Tell me what you have done."

So Jonathan told him, "I tasted a little honey with the end of my staff. And now I must die!"

Saul said, "May God deal with me, be it ever so severely, if you do not die, Jonathan."

But the men said to Saul, "Should Jonathan die—he who has brought about this great deliverance in Israel? Never! As surely as the LORD lives, not a hair of his head will fall to the ground, for he did this today with God's help." So the men rescued Jonathan, and he was not put to death. (vv. 38–45)

How shocked Saul must have been at the outcome of this session of casting lots. It is obvious that the leaders of the army knew when to keep their mouths shut because none of them were speaking up until the situation became dire. Finally they did speak up and rescued Jonathan.

It seems that Saul would have gone through with the execution of his own son, for his own reputation's sake, had the troops not stopped him. No doubt he regretted his rash words: "Even if it lies with my son Jonathan, he must die." Yet how far would he have gone if the officers had not intervened?

It may say a lot for Jonathan's character that the officers were willing to speak up for him against his father the king and commander of the army. Obviously they were reluctant to do so before they had to, but they were unwilling to see this brave young man die needlessly and stopped the foolishness there.

The end of 1 Samuel 14 gives us a bit more insight into Saul's character.

After Saul had assumed rule over Israel, he fought against their enemies on every side: Moab, the Ammonites, Edom, the kings of Zobah, and the Philistines. Wherever he turned, he inflicted punishment on them. He fought valiantly and defeated the Amalekites, delivering Israel from the hands of those who had plundered them.

. . . All the days of Saul there was bitter war with the Philistines, and whenever Saul saw a mighty or brave man, he took him into his service. (vv. 47–52)

Saul was a valiant soldier and successful in battle. He carried out the role he had been given. It is not that Saul was an utter failure or that he was lazy or unwilling to do his job. The people probably saw him as a fairly good, if not a great, leader. But God saw him very differently as we will continue to see.

That last verse is very revealing in light of the topic of this chapter. Saul was very effective in choosing his staff. He could evaluate people well. He knew what he needed to win wars, and he successfully recruited valiant, mighty, and brave men. Then he used them up to accomplish the task at hand.

Let's compare Saul's approach in caring for those who worked for him with David's approach to leadership.

What Was It like to Work for David?

David had a very interesting beginning to his leadership. It was certainly neither ideal nor easy because he was on the run as a fugitive and criminal when he began to recruit people to join him.

First Samuel 18–20 is the account of David's ascension and Saul's decline. Several times the Scriptures speak of Saul's growing fear and jealousy of David. David had success in battle and with people; God was with him but had left Saul (1 Samuel 18:12).

Then we read the stories of David fleeing for his life from Saul and all the ways that God protected David and frustrated Saul's attempts to destroy him. David spent years in exile, because Saul was ruthlessly trying to destroy him, to prevent him from taking over the kingdom.

It is in these stories that we find out what kind of people David inherited as his staff. Let's turn to 1 Samuel 22:1–2: "David left Gath and escaped to the cave of Adullam. When his brothers and his father's household heard about it, they went down to him there. All those who were in distress or in debt or discontented gathered around him, and he became their commander. About four hundred men were with him."

Unlike Saul, David didn't have the luxury of choosing the brightest and the best, or as the Scripture puts it, "Whenever Saul saw a mighty or brave man, he took him into his service" (1 Samuel 14:52). No, David got all of the leftovers; in fact, he got the real problems.

Do you ever feel that is a good description of the people who work for you? I know leaders who do. Often they take on the role of pastor or leader of a Christian ministry, only to find out they have inherited a mess, a group of people who no one in his or her right mind would ever choose to have as followers.

What do you do in that situation? Sometimes in the West we can fire many of them and replace them with others more to our liking; but that is a rarity. Usually when we find ourselves in this situation, we are dealing with people in our parish or congregation, and we don't get to choose who is there. Other times we lead volunteers, and we get whoever comes. In some countries the laws protect workers more than they do leaders, and firing someone is not only undesirable, but also virtually impossible.

David was in that position. He had no room to be choosy. He was stuck with those who showed up in the cave, and he knew it.

Actually for David it even got worse. We find that Saul killed everyone associated with the first place David turned for refuge: the town of Nob. Saul executed eighty-five priests of the Lord and even all the men, women, and children of Nob, because Ahimelek innocently believed David's false story and supplied him with bread and a sword. David accepted the blame for this when a young man who escaped ran to David for help: "But one son of Ahimelek son of Ahitub, named Abiathar, escaped and fled to join David. He told David that Saul had killed the priests of the LORD. Then David said to Abiathar, 'That day, when Doeg the Edomite was there, I knew he would be sure to tell Saul. I am responsible for the death of your whole family. Stay with me; don't be afraid. The man who wants to take your life is trying to kill me too. You will be safe with me" (1 Samuel 22:20–23).

So David had all of those in distress, debt, and discontented, as well as a refugee. These men followed David for years of torment and battle. They were constantly on the run from Saul, while also facing battles with the enemy forces from the surrounding nations. They were men without a country who had to live by their wits.

An example is the story of the burning of Ziklag. This was the city that the king of Gath gave to David for him and his troops to occupy: "So David and the six hundred men with him left and went over to Achish son of Maok king of Gath. David and his men settled in Gath with Achish. Each man had his family with him, and David had his two wives: Ahinoam of Jezreel and Abigail of Carmel, the widow of Nabal" (1 Samuel 27:2–3).

David had collected six hundred men, and with them are all of their loved ones. Fortunately the king of Gath, one of the Philistine lords, had given the city of Ziklag to them to live in.

But things soon took a turn for the worse. When David and the men returned to Ziklag after an aborted attempt to fight with the Philistines against Israel, they found the entire city had been sacked, burned, and everyone carried off into captivity by the Amalekites. They lost everything they held dear, and David's men were ready to kill him.

When David and his men reached Ziklag, they found it destroyed by fire and their wives and sons and daughters taken captive. So David and his men wept aloud until they had no strength left to weep. David's two wives had been captured—Ahinoam of Jezreel and Abigail, the widow of Nabal of Carmel. David was greatly distressed because the men were talking of stoning him; each one was bitter in spirit because of his sons and daughters. But David found strength in the LORD his God. (1 Samuel 30:3–6)

Over and over again David was faced with impossible odds and horrible conditions. Here he had been rejected not only by Israel but also by the Philistines. His only home had been destroyed, those he loved captured, and he had no idea of their fate. His men turned on him and discussed stoning him. What was his response? He found strength in the Lord his God.

I love the phrase "David found strength in the LORD his God." Where do you find your strength when the bottom falls out of everything you have been building? Where do you turn for comfort, solace, and help? Many of us get angry with God at that point. We stomp our feet like little children when things don't go our way and shake our fists at God in anger. Others of us just turn to something to soothe the pain, like alcohol, drugs, sex, or entertainment. We want to forget our dreams that have been dashed, forget the pain that has resulted, and forget that we ever cared.

But David turned to God for strength and for answers. He didn't presume and act rashly. He didn't try to tell God what God had to do, but he sincerely inquired of the Lord about what should happen next. And God answered.

Then David said to Abiathar the priest, the son of Ahimelek, "Bring me the ephod." Abiathar brought it to him, and David inquired of the LORD, "Shall I pursue this raiding party? Will I overtake them?"

"Pursue them," he answered. "You will certainly overtake them and succeed in the rescue."

. . . David recovered everything the Amalekites had taken, including his two wives. Nothing was missing: young or old, boy or girl, plunder or anything else they had taken. David brought everything back. (1 Samuel 30:7–19)

So God restored to David everything precious to him and his men. God's goodness once again prevailed.

These men of David's, the distressed, debtors, discontented, and refugees stuck with David throughout the rest of his life, through bad times and good. As you read 1 and 2 Samuel you will find the exploits of David's men. In fact, at some point they are no longer referred to as the distressed, debtors, discontented, and refugees, but they become David's mighty men.

In 2 Samuel 23:8–39 are some of the stories of David's chief men. They were loyal, able to do great exploits, and were followers of God. These were not a different batch of people which David picked up later. Rather these are the very same men who gathered around David in the cave at Adullam. These men grew from discontents into mighty warriors of God from having lived and worked with David for up to forty years.

Living and working with David was certainly not an easy journey. We know that because of some of the stories like what happened at Ziklag. Yet these men grew into their potential by being followers of David. Why? What did David do that enabled these men to mature?

Maybe there is a strong clue in David's last recorded words. Let's look at those recorded in 2 Samuel 23: 2–4:

> The Spirit of the LORD spoke through me;
>> his word was on my tongue.
> The God of Israel spoke,
>> the Rock of Israel said to me:
> "When one rules over people in righteousness,
>> when he rules in the fear of God,

he is like the light of morning at sunrise

on a cloudless morning,

like the brightness after rain

that brings the grass from the earth."

Righteous leadership results in people growing into their potential, in fact, beyond their potential!

Let's Compare Saul and David

So there you have it. Saul picked the brightest and the best to serve under him. He chose men of bravery and strength. Then he used them to accomplish his purposes, and eventually they all were killed in battle. We do not come away from any of the stories of Saul's life and battles with a sense that the men with him grew into their potential or became better through working closely with him.

David, on the other hand, inherited the dregs of society as his staff and then lived with them and fought with them. Through their exposure to David's life of faith and fear of God, they became mighty warriors of God.

This presents an interesting comparison between leaders whom God rejects versus those in whom he takes great pleasure. Really, there is no comparison. How well have you done at enabling those who work with you to grow into their potential?

I have had the rare privilege of working for more than one leader who genuinely cared more about my welfare than his own. One of those leaders had a habit of saying to me, "How can I be sure you are successful and fulfilled?" The other one never used those words but always acted them out.

Each of those leaders entrusted me with responsibilities that I wasn't sure I had the capacity to carry out. Then they not only gave me the responsibility but also mentored me and walked beside me, carefully ensuring my success.

The result in my life has been the wonderful experience of doing more than I ever believed I could possibly do. I have had opportunities handed to me to grow and explore. I have been pushed and encouraged to succeed. I have been mentored and cared for so that even when I made mistakes, together we found ways to salvage what we could and learn from those mistakes so that at least I never made exactly the same one again.

Unfortunately, too few of us in Christian work have served under the kind of leaders I have. Too many of us can identify with Saul's fighting men. And while we cannot change what happened to us as followers, as leaders we have the opportunity to be like David.

You can ensure that those under you are enabled and fulfilled. You have that power. How are you using it? Does your leadership look more like Saul's or David's?

Questions for Reflection:

- Are you more concerned for your image or for the welfare of your staff and volunteers?
- Look back over your leadership. Did the people who worked under you grow into mighty men and women of God, or did you simply use them up and wear them out to accomplish your goals? Think of specific examples of either.

5

QUESTION 3:
Do I Put My Interests before God's Interests?

In the 1980s in the United States there were several high-profile Christian leaders who fell into horrific sin. Although sexual immorality was involved, the majority of the messes they created involved money and power, corruption and greed over a long period of time. Of course this was not the first time this had happened in history, but, maybe because of the advent of more media coverage, these became major news stories.

At the time I was serving as the lawyer for a number of other high-profile Christian leaders and their ministries, wonderful men and women of God whom it was a privilege to serve. I wanted to understand how leaders in Christian ministry could end up in such a mess. How did they get there? Were there signs I should be looking for to help protect my clients from failing? I was one of the few people who understood all of their business dealings, and I wanted to be sure that I did not become complicit in failure.

As I read the coverage of these men who had once been such powerful forces for the gospel, a theme became very evident. These leaders had convinced themselves that the end justified the means.

Their failures began by trying to relieve financial pressures with small decisions that were not quite right. Then they covered up those decisions with other bad decisions "for the sake of the ministry." Small decisions became downward spirals of ongoing fraud, theft, and every form of corrupt business practice, which they justified by thinking it was more important to keep their ministries going.

This pattern of sin that uses God-given position and power to promote personal interests and reputation while disregarding God's law is something that God truly despises. Of course we know that God hates all sin, yet he is quick to forgive and forget our sins when we sincerely repent. God loves redemption. It is his specialty.

So let us look carefully at the failures of both Saul and David. From God's reaction to each we can learn a great deal. What did God see in each of their hearts? Why did he find Saul's sin so repulsive, and why did he forgive and restore David so completely? It is critical that we try to understand this and then try to learn from the lives of these two kings of Israel, appointed by God, anointed by God, and equipped by God.

Saul's Failure and God's Response

The story of Saul's final failure to please God is really not about a huge decision to intentionally sin. Rather it is about a series of small decisions of not taking God seriously, of being only half-devoted to God, of being more concerned with self-preservation than with God's heart, God's interests, and God's ways.

It is a story that in some ways we could find reasonable on Saul's part. In fact, were it not for God's response to Saul's actions, we might be lulled into thinking they weren't all serious and were arguably justifiable. But we would be horribly wrong and sadly misinformed.

Let's pick up the story at the beginning of 1 Samuel 15, where Saul received his instructions.

> Samuel said to Saul, "I am the one the LORD sent to anoint you king over his people Israel; so listen now to the message from the LORD. This is what the LORD Almighty says: 'I will punish the Amalekites for what they did to Israel when they waylaid them as they came up from Egypt. Now go, attack the Amalekites and totally destroy all that belongs to them. Do not spare them; put to death men and women, children and infants, cattle and sheep, camels and donkeys.'" (vv. 1–4)

Samuel went to Saul with a clear word from God. Some of us as Christian leaders long for clear instructions from God. At times we wonder if we are doing the right thing or if we have something confused. But Saul did not have to be concerned about that. Samuel made his case to help Saul grasp the gravity of this command from God, and then he clearly spelled out what was to be done.

In response, Saul gathered the troops and attacked the Amalekites, just as directed. However, he did not carry out the task according to the instructions. Let's read what Saul did and did not do: "Then Saul attacked the Amalekites all the way from Havilah to Shur, near the eastern border of Egypt. He took Agag king of the Amalekites alive, and all his people he totally destroyed with the sword. But Saul and the army spared Agag and the best of the sheep and cattle, the fat calves and lambs—everything that was good. These they were unwilling to destroy completely, but everything that was despised and weak they totally destroyed" (vv. 7–9).

Do you see a problem here? Saul attacked the Amalekites. So far, so good, right? But then he began making decisions that did not match his instructions. He left the king alive and all of the best animals. Saul was "unwilling to destroy completely" everything that was good.

God's reaction was swift and thorough. He spoke to Samuel, and the words are chilling: "Then the word of the LORD came to Samuel: 'I regret that I have made Saul king, because he has turned away from me and has not carried out my instructions.' Samuel was angry, and he cried out to the LORD all that night" (vv. 10–11).

God said that he regretted making Saul king. What an amazing statement. How is it even possible for the all-powerful, almighty, all-knowing God of the universe to feel regret?

Arguably, or at least in this example, it is when we, his chosen leaders, fail to obey. We do have free will, and we do have the option to obey or not to obey. We can even delude ourselves into thinking we have obeyed when in fact we have not. Just listen to Saul's response when Samuel confronted him with the truth.

> When Samuel reached him, Saul said, "The LORD bless you! I have carried out the LORD's instructions."
>
> But Samuel said, "What then is this bleating of sheep in my ears? What is this lowing of cattle that I hear?"
>
> Saul answered, "The soldiers brought them from the Amalekites; they spared the best of the sheep and cattle to sacrifice to the LORD your God, but we totally destroyed the rest." (vv. 13–15)

Saul seems unperturbed by Samuel's arrival. He excitedly announced his wonderful success and obedience and then argued with Samuel when confronted. Saul even explained and attempted to shift the blame by saying that the soldiers decided to spare the best of the animals, but only so that they could sacrifice them to the Lord. What a great idea—right?

Then follows another exchange where Samuel pointed out Saul's failure and the ramifications of it, and Saul argued with him again.

> "Enough!" Samuel said to Saul. "Let me tell you what the LORD said to me last night."

"Tell me," Saul replied.

Samuel said, "Although you were once small in your own eyes, did you not become the head of the tribes of Israel? The Lord anointed you king over Israel. And he sent you on a mission, saying, 'Go and completely destroy those wicked people, the Amalekites; make war on them until you have wiped them out.' Why did you not obey the Lord? Why did you pounce on the plunder and do evil in the eyes of the Lord?"

"But I did obey the Lord," Saul said. "I went on the mission the Lord assigned me. I completely destroyed the Amalekites and brought back Agag their king. The soldiers took sheep and cattle from the plunder, the best of what was devoted to God, in order to sacrifice them to the Lord your God at Gilgal." (vv. 16–21)

Denial and excuses were all that Samuel got from Saul the second time he was confronted with the facts. How many times do we try to justify our disobedience to ourselves, others, and even to God when we know we have fallen short?

Obviously God and Samuel both knew that this was not some heartfelt desire on Saul's part to present a gift to God. While we may be able to justify our failures to ourselves and maybe even to others, God knows our hearts, and we cannot con him with our eloquent phrases or denials.

And here we come to the crux of the matter—the heart. Samuel pointed out, in one of the most eloquent dissertations in the Bible, what really matters to God, while confronting Saul for the third time with his sin.

But Samuel replied:

"Does the Lord delight in burnt offerings and sacrifices
as much as in obeying the Lord?

To obey is better than sacrifice,

and to heed is better than the fat of rams.

For rebellion is like the sin of divination,

and arrogance like the evil of idolatry.

Because you have rejected the word of the LORD,

he has rejected you as king." (vv. 22–23)

Samuel told Saul that this was not about animals being alive or offered as sacrifices. This was about pride. Saul was saying that he was obeying God when actually he was doing things his own way and doing exactly what he pleased. Arrogance becomes idolatry when we put ourselves on the throne in the place of God.

Back in verse 12 of this chapter, a verse we skipped over earlier, is an amazing little clue to what had gone wrong here. When Samuel was looking for Saul, he went to meet him and found that Saul had gone over to Carmel, where Saul had "set up a monument in his own honor."

Leadership always comes with power, and it always comes with opportunities for pride to creep in and take over. We as leaders receive credit for whatever good happens within our organizations or churches, no matter who actually does the work.

There is always the danger of believing the good things that are written about us or that people say. We love the idea that we are important, critical, successful, and valued. We love anything that makes us feel secure in ourselves, because then we can be independent of God.

In fact, this is the very root of the issue of burnout in ministry. We take on tasks that God never intended for us to do. We work beyond the hours he has set for us to work and fail to take the Sabbath seriously. We drive our people to do more than they should be doing. And we do it because it feels good. It feeds our egos that we are so important and busy and that everyone needs us and wants our time. Our affections become misplaced, and we are so busy listening to everyone else that we fail to listen to God.

I had a telling phone conversation with another Christian leader recently:

"Hi, Mike, how are you doing?"

"Oh, I'm okay, but I am just so busy! It seems like every day has more to do in it than I can possibly do. How about you?"

"Oh, that pretty well sums up my life these days. It seems like there are more e-mails than I can manage and meetings and phone calls. Well, it just seems like everyone is demanding something and that they need it urgently. I should be able to manage better, but it is so hard to do."

"Yes, I've just read a new book on managing your time, and I think you should read it, Jane. It really had some great clues for busy leaders."

"Oh, I'd love to get the title of that—but then I'd have to make time to read it, wouldn't I?! (laughter) Well, talk to you soon then . . . "

What a horrible conversation! How ridiculous that we believe God would give us more than we can get done. Isn't it abundantly clear that if we find ourselves in this situation that somehow we have completely missed what God has for us? We should repent and ask God's forgiveness for being busy with things he never asked us to do, and especially ask forgiveness for loving the fact that we are so important!

Let's get back to Saul's response because he finally admitted guilt and reluctantly repented—sort of.

> Then Saul said to Samuel, "I have sinned. I violated the Lord's command and your instructions. I was afraid of the men and so I gave in to them. Now I beg you, forgive my sin and come back with me, so that I may worship the Lord."

But Samuel said to him, "I will not go back with you. You have rejected the word of the LORD, and the LORD has rejected you as king over Israel!"

As Samuel turned to leave, Saul caught hold of the hem of his robe, and it tore. Samuel said to him, "The LORD has torn the kingdom of Israel from you today and has given it to one of your neighbors—to one better than you. He who is the Glory of Israel does not lie or change his mind; for he is not a human being, that he should change his mind." (vv. 24–29)

Finally Saul admitted his failure. But then he shifted blame again and said that his actions resulted from fear of his men. In other words, he was more afraid of men than of God. We get the feeling that he was sorry he got caught, but not sorry for the sin.

In fact, Saul's next statement is even more damning: "'I have sinned. But please honor me before the elders of my people and before Israel; come back with me, so that I may worship the LORD your God.' So Samuel went back with Saul, and Saul worshiped the LORD" (vv. 30–31).

He admitted his sin in response to Samuel's speech and didn't try to make a case for why God should not reject him. Instead he asked Samuel to honor him before the people anyway! Obviously if Samuel walked away at this point Saul would lose credibility; and he didn't want to risk that. It seems that he didn't comprehend that he had already lost his position because God had rejected him; he was still worried about what others thought of him.

Notice the language in the phrase about worshiping God. Saul said, "So that I may worship the LORD *your* God" (v. 30, emphasis added). Did he really mean that? Why did he say, "The LORD your God," rather than "The LORD our God" or "The LORD my God"? Was it because he knew that God was not really his Lord?

What about you? Who is your audience? Who are you trying to please? Who do you believe holds your future in their hands?

I once had a friend who had played a major leadership role in a very large denomination for many years. He voluntarily stepped down from that position to enjoy a sabbatical season before moving on to another role. Surprisingly he found himself miserable. He was lonely, irritated, and totally at loose ends. He had thought he would relish having unlimited time alone with the Lord and for study, but instead he found that he didn't know how to spend time with the Lord anymore. He missed his friends, his cars, and people vying for his time and hanging on his every word. He found he missed power and position.

In this story Samuel did comply and return with Saul, and they worshiped. Then the story tells us that Samuel's next act was to kill Agag, the Amalekite king Saul had let live. Samuel was a prophet and priest who not only delivered the word of the Lord to leaders but also, at times, delivered the judgment of God.

The last verse of this chapter is probably the most troubling of the whole chapter: "Until the day Samuel died, he did not go to see Saul again, though Samuel mourned for him. And the LORD regretted that he had made Saul king over Israel" (v. 35).

Samuel was heartbroken over this turn of events because he loved God so much and understood what God wanted. I believe that Samuel knew what kind of leader Saul could have been. The fact that he "mourned" for him gives us a sense of the deep degree of loss that Samuel and God must have felt.

Saul's leadership was a tragedy. While he generally did what was asked of him, he failed to do it in the way God desired. There was a lack of desire to please God fully, and in its place was the practice of ensuring that he maintained his position, his status, and his role. Saul's leadership was a loss, a waste of precious resources, people, and time. And God "regretted that he had made Saul king over Israel."

David's Failure and God's Response

Let's turn from Saul and take a look at David. David was a man after God's heart. His desire was to please God. He constantly sought to obey God's commands and did it with great joy. He obeyed out of a deep and passionate love for God. He wanted to bring God joy more than anything else, more than he wanted position, power, and throne.

But David was not perfect. In fact, he had some enormous failures. Yet they were the exceptions to the rule of a life of passionate obedience. The pattern of his life was marvelous obedience with joy.

Let us look at David's famous departure into lust, adultery, and murder and then look at a couple of examples of his normal pattern of obedience with joy. Here we will find the lessons for our lives as leaders. Let's explore together why God forgave David so completely and remained so genuinely pleased with his leadership.

Here lie some of the biggest clues to genuine success in leadership. There is reassurance here for those who have failed and then genuinely repented and sought God's forgiveness. There is great encouragement for those trying to please God out of hearts of love. There are frightening lessons for those who slide into using leadership for their own egos, while trying to justify their behaviors to God.

Let's start with what is undeniably a horrendous series of actions of David. If you want to read them, they are found in 2 Samuel 11–12. We will not spend a lot of time recounting David's sins, but merely say that it all seems to have begun when he failed to go to war and sent Joab instead. While hanging around the palace one day, David saw Bathsheba bathing, lusted after her, sent for her, and committed adultery with her. When she became pregnant, he tried to cover it up by bringing her husband, Uriah, home from the battlefield, getting him drunk, and sending him home to sleep with his wife. Uriah refused to sleep with his wife when the rest of his colleagues were on the battlefield. So in desperation David had him killed by ordering him and others sent to the frontlines of the battle and having the troops withdraw from them. So here we have adultery and premeditated murder along with a laundry list of more minor crimes like lust, lying, deceit, collusion, and unnecessary collateral damage in battle. Certainly a horrible list of sins by anyone, especially God's chosen leader. And God does not tolerate sin.

Chapter 11 ends with the phrase that what David had done "displeased the LORD," and God sent Nathan the prophet to confront him. Nathan's way of communicating to David is riveting. He told David a parable that was so outrageous that David declared that the rich man in the story must die. Then Nathan pointed out that David was the rich man in the story. Then Nathan told him the punishment for his sins: "Then Nathan said to David, 'You are the man! This is what the LORD, the God of Israel, says: "I anointed you king over Israel, and I delivered you from the hand of Saul. I gave your master's house to you, and your master's wives into your arms. I gave you the house of Israel and Judah. And if all this had been too little, I would have given you even more"'" (2 Samuel 12:7–8).

Nathan's message began with a heart-rending account of how much God had given to David. It sounds like a father's heart for his son. God even said, "And if all this had been too little, I would have given you even more." Can you hear God's heart breaking?

> Why did you despise the word of the LORD by doing what is evil in his eyes? You struck down Uriah the Hittite with the sword and took his wife to be your own. You killed him with the sword of the Ammonites. Now, therefore, the sword will never depart from your house, because you despised me and took the wife of Uriah the Hittite to be your own.
>
> This is what the LORD says: "Out of your own household I am going to bring calamity on you. Before your very eyes I will take your wives and give them to

one who is close to you, and he will sleep with your wives in broad daylight. You did it in secret, but I will do this thing in broad daylight before all Israel." (vv. 9–12)

The results of David's sin would be horrible and long term. We have the story, so we know how painfully it plays out. Everything Nathan predicted here did take place later in David's life. This would haunt him for the rest of his life. This was not because God desired for that to be the case but because there are always consequences to our actions. God forgives, heals, and redeems, but he does not magically reverse what our choices have set in motion here on earth. We usually have to live with the outcomes of our sinful behaviors long after the sin has been forgiven and we have moved on.

Thankfully David immediately acknowledged his sin and re-pented, because Nathan continued: "The LORD has taken away your sin. You are not going to die. But because by doing this you have shown utter contempt for the LORD, the son born to you will die" (vv. 13–14).

What follows in verses 15–23 is a fascinating account of David's actions in response to this word about the child dying:

> After Nathan had gone home, the LORD struck the child that Uriah's wife had borne to David, and he became ill. David pleaded with God for the child. He fasted and spent the nights lying in sackcloth on the ground. The elders of his household stood beside him to get him up from the ground, but he refused, and he would not eat any food with them.
>
> On the seventh day the child died. David's atten-dants were afraid to tell him that the child was dead, for they thought, "While the child was still living, he wouldn't listen to us when we spoke to him. How can we now tell him the child is dead? He may do something desperate."

David noticed that his attendants were whispering among themselves, and he realized the child was dead. "Is the child dead?" he asked.

"Yes," they replied, "he is dead."

Then David got up from the ground. After he had washed, put on lotions and changed his clothes, he went into the house of the LORD and worshiped. Then he went to his own house, and at his request they served him food, and he ate.

His attendants asked him, "Why are you acting this way? While the child was alive, you fasted and wept, but now that the child is dead, you get up and eat!"

He answered, "While the child was still alive, I fasted and wept. I thought, 'Who knows? The LORD may be gracious to me and let the child live.' But now that he is dead, why should I go on fasting? Can I bring him back again? I will go to him, but he will not return to me."

These are the responses of a man with a deep knowledge of God and an abiding relationship with him. David had such a profound understanding of God's character that he knew that God might extend grace and let the child live. But that was not to be. Instead the next verses tell us that David comforted Bathsheba, made love to her again, and the resulting child was Solomon. God's response was typical of his character as Redeemer: "Then David comforted his wife Bathsheba, and he went to her and made love to her. She gave birth to a son, and they named him Solomon. The LORD loved him; and because the LORD loved him, he sent word through Nathan the prophet to name him Jedidiah" (vv. 24–25).

God loved Solomon. He did not hold it against him that he was the child of a marriage that had the wrong genesis. Instead his overwhelming love for David came through in this pronouncement of love for Solomon.

God forgave David completely. That is something that we as human beings are rarely capable of, and therefore we cannot believe that God is either. We always have a tendency to project onto others what we would do in a similar situation. So often in the church we do not let people forget their past, but God is able to do so completely when we repent and seek his forgiveness. Oh, that the church could reflect that part of God's character! What an amazing testimony it would be.

Returning to David's story, the final verses of 2 Samuel 12 recount that Joab, the commander of the army, sent David a message saying that a city was about to be captured and if David didn't get there, Joab would wrongly get the credit.

So David mustered the troops, joined the battle, and stayed in the fight throughout the rest of the fighting season. It seems clear that his choice to not go to war when he was supposed to initially led to the series of sins that escalated so horribly. His decision to return to war in this case seems to signal obedience to God and confirm David's turning away from sin.

David's response to God when confronted with his sin by the prophet Nathan was very different from Saul's response to God when confronted with his sin by the prophet Samuel. Saul blustered, denied, shifted blame, and seems to have been genuinely sorry only for the fact that he got caught. In contrast, David quickly and clearly accepted the blame for his failure. David's response gives us insight into his relationship with God.

This reminds me of a leader I met in Africa who came to a seminar on servant leadership. At the end of the first morning session he sat down with a colleague of mine, Nora, and said, "I am so grateful that no one else from my church was here today!" Somewhat confused, Nora asked him why he would say that. "Because," he said, "I feel like someone has taken off all of my clothes and I have been exposed for who I really am—a Big Boss! If anyone from my church had been here today and heard that case study, they would have recognized me immediately. I have failed so miserably as a leader, and I want to change. I know these courses are expensive, and I may have to sell my car to be able to attend them all; but I am going to do whatever it takes to change. I want to change. I have to change!"

God loves a contrite heart. He loves it when we completely and unequivocally confess our sins, repent, and turn to him. We may put off confession because of embarrassment, because we do not want others to see us for who we really are. But if we humble ourselves, confess to those who need to know, repent, and turn from our sin, God is quick to forgive us.

God finds no pleasure in holding our sin over us or reminding us of past failures. No matter what we have done, there is forgiveness available and complete redemption waiting. David's story is one in which any leader who has failed and genuinely repented and turned away from his sin can find great comfort.

David's Normal Pattern of Putting God's Interests First

Let's turn to two other incidents in David's life that are much more typical of his behavior. They each give us some sense of David's heart and his abiding relationship with God. Of special interest here is that David never seems to try to build his own reputation or look after primarily his own power or position. This seems to be at the heart of the difference between him and Saul.

In 2 Samuel 6 there is a story of David dancing before the Lord with all his might in a linen ephod as the ark of the covenant entered the city of Jerusalem. His wife Michal did not approve and thought he had embarrassed not only himself but also her through his unseemly behavior. His response is instructive.

> When David returned home to bless his household, Michal daughter of Saul came out to meet him and said, "How the king of Israel has distinguished himself today, going around half-naked in full view of the slave girls of

his servants as any vulgar fellow would!"

David said to Michal, "It was before the LORD, who chose me rather than your father or anyone from his house when he appointed me ruler over the LORD's people Israel—I will celebrate before the LORD. I will become even more undignified than this, and I will be humiliated in my own eyes. But by these slave girls you spoke of, I will be held in honor."

And Michal daughter of Saul had no children to the day of her death. (vv. 20–23)

David was happy to be undignified and humbled before the Lord in public, no matter what anyone else thought. And he let Michal know that while she might think less of him for his behavior, others would not. He was very secure in his wholehearted abandonment in worship before God.

Another exchange, in 2 Samuel 7, between David and the Lord is precious in its depth. David reflected on the fact that God had given him rest on all sides from his enemies and had given him a beautiful palace, but the ark of the covenant was still in a tent. Nathan agreed with him and told him to go forward with any plans on his mind. But then Nathan had a dream from the Lord that contravened that idea, and he reported these things to David.

God promised David many beautiful things in that dream, including the promise that he would never take the kingdom away from him as he did Saul. The remainder of that chapter is David's prayer back to God, filled with a heart of obedience, love, and gratitude. This is an exchange filled with love, understanding, and deep relationship between a man and God.

Over and over again, as we will see, David held his leadership position lightly. He never felt the need to protect it; in fact, in the early days he refused the opportunities to kill Saul and take the kingship that had been promised to him. Later he refused to fight for the position when Absalom took it away from him.

David relaxed in God's sovereignty and simply trusted God with his life: "O Sovereign Lord, you are God! Your words are trustworthy, and you have promised these good things to your servant. . . . For you, O Sovereign Lord, have spoken, and with your blessing the house of your servant will be blessed forever" (1 Samuel 7:28–29). David did not need to compromise to bring about God's will. If God wanted David to remain king, God himself would bring that to pass. David consistently put God's interests first and trusted him completely. When he did fail miserably, he transparently admitted his guilt, repented, and turned away from sin. Then he returned wholeheartedly to embrace God's sovereignty and his ways.

Saul, on the other hand, never really did seem to understand the purpose of his leadership role. He never really seemed to put God first and build a relationship with him. He regularly went his own way, especially when under the stress of possibly losing his kingdom or the loyalty of his men. Even though he continued to fulfill the role of king for forty-two years, he often put his own interests first, not fully obeying God's commands, not fully trusting God with his life and position.

Does your leadership look more like Saul's or David's?

Questions for Reflection:

- How often has your leadership grieved God because you followed your own ideas instead of completely obeying him?
- How quick are you to repent, or do you easily find ways to justify and bluster when confronted with your sin?
- Are you honestly more interested in the welfare of God's kingdom or yours?

QUESTION 4:
Do I Lead with Integrity?

Who are you when no one is looking? Are you the same person when you are alone as you are when in public, up on the platform? Integrity means behaving in the same way all the time, whether or not others can see you. And it is one of the greatest challenges of leadership, especially for those whose influence grows and who become well-known public figures.

For nearly three years I was a college professor. I taught subjects relating to Christian missions at a small Christian college in the northeast United States. I have to admit that I was very intimidated by the role initially but soon learned to totally enjoy it. I built relationships with many of the students and loved all of the honest exchanges during classes.

In my second semester, I found that I had one student, a young man, who sat at the back of my classes and refused to engage in the dialogue. He even seemed a bit surly with me, and I could tell he didn't like me. But I could not figure out why.

I am not one of those women who need to have everyone love them; that's not my personality. But over the days and weeks of having this young man sit in the back of my class and scowl, it really troubled me. I finally worked up the courage to try to find out what I had done to offend him. So one day after class I asked him if he would go have a cup of coffee with me; and, somewhat to my surprise, he readily agreed.

We walked into the commons, ordered our steaming hot cups of coffee, and as we sat down, I began to ask him some general questions about his life, background, and why he had an interest in missions. I was just trying to break the ice and get to know him a little before trying to delve into the subject of why he so obviously detested me.

After just a few minutes he volunteered the fact that I reminded him of his mother. Aha! I could tell we were getting somewhere as I tried not to be offended that he thought I could be old enough to be his mother—although of course I was!

When I asked about his father, his face went dark. He said he didn't really know his father too well because his father and mother were divorced. Then he went on to say that his father was a pastor. In fact, at that point he laughed mirthlessly and said, "Well, actually all of my fathers are pastors. Mom's married five of them, though she is currently in the process of divorcing this last one! Yep, I've been a preacher's kid in five different churches with five different dads. That's got to be some kind of record I suppose, doesn't it?"

I have found that many young people who grew up in the evangelical church have no respect for it. In fact, many have little interest in attending church, but have a great deal of interest in true community and what they perceive to be true spirituality. They have an interest in anything that seems to them to be genuine and focused on loving Jesus. They often draw a distinction between that and church.

Is it because of what they have seen? Is it because the divorce rate for Christians in the United States is as high as it is for non-

Christians? Is it because they have seen too much duplicity in our lives as Christian leaders? It is because of the loss of integrity?

I can remember a few years ago working closely with a number of Christian leaders who were ten to twenty years older than I. Several of them were struggling with adult children who were in deep trouble. These leaders kept asking themselves if it was their fault. All shared with regret the fact that they wished they had spent more time with their children when they were young and the children wanted to be with them.

I have never in my thirty years of ministry met Christian leaders who felt they spent too much time with their families or regret the time they took out of ministry to spend with family members. On the other hand, I have met many who regret not spending enough time with their families and some who feel that they sacrificed their families wrongly on the altar of ministry.

Saul's Lack of Integrity

Saul's story does not get better with time. In other words, as he drew toward the close of his tenure as king, he continued to struggle with the same issues. He was fearful, insecure, and desperate for God only when he needed something from him; and he still had the menacing Philistines on the borders.

Let's pick up his story in 1 Samuel 28:3–5 to discover Saul's level of integrity.

> Now Samuel was dead, and all Israel had mourned for him and buried him in his own town of Ramah. Saul had expelled the mediums and spiritists from the land.
>
> The Philistines assembled and came and set up camp at Shunem, while Saul gathered all Israel and set up camp at Gilboa. When Saul saw the Philistine army, he was afraid; terror filled his heart.

Samuel was dead. This in itself must have been traumatic for Saul. He may not have liked Samuel, who was his nemesis in many ways; but he was the one God had used to anoint Saul for leadership. Samuel was the one who always told Saul what God wanted him to do. In fact, Samuel was the only source of comfort and direction that Saul had, as he seemed to have no relationship with God.

Saul had expelled the mediums and spiritists from the land. We can assume this was a positive thing he had done in response to God's direction to cleanse the land of those who got their power and direction from Satan.

Once again the Philistines assembled for battle, and Israel was no match for them as usual. Had Saul learned through more than forty years of leadership to trust God? Had he developed faith to believe that God would protect his people? Apparently not, as we find that "terror filled his heart."

It is never a crime to be afraid. Fear does not equal sin. What we do about our fear is what matters. Let's see what Saul did: "He inquired of the LORD, but the LORD did not answer him by dreams or Urim or prophets. Saul then said to his attendants, 'Find me a woman who is a medium, so I may go and inquire of her'" (vv. 6–7). He was told there was one in Endor.

This is a classic example of taking things into our own hands, of compromising all that we know to be right in order to get what we want. Saul wanted information wherever he could find it—in this case from a medium or witch, which he knew to be against God's will.

> So Saul disguised himself, putting on other clothes, and at night he and two men went to the woman. "Consult a spirit for me," he said, "and bring up for me the one I name."
>
> But the woman said to him, "Surely you know what Saul has done. He has cut off the mediums and spiritists from the land. Why have you set a trap for my life to

bring about my death?"

Saul swore to her by the LORD, "As surely as the LORD lives, you will not be punished for this."

Then the woman asked, "Whom shall I bring up for you?"

"Bring up Samuel," he said.

When the woman saw Samuel, she cried out at the top of her voice and said to Saul, "Why have you deceived me? You are Saul!" (vv. 8–12)

Some people in Western culture are too sophisticated to believe in witches, medium, and spiritists. They believe that such things exist only as fictional characters in children's stories. Most people in other cultures do not make that mistake. They know full well the power of the dark side, and it is not uncommon for many Christian leaders in those cultures to try to appease both sides.

I recently met with a friend in a West African nation who was celebrating that a political leader had come to him for counsel about his inauguration plans. This leader told my friend that he wanted to honor God throughout his inauguration and would not do the traditional rituals. Much to my friend's surprise and joy this political leader stood by his word.

My friend went to be with this political leader throughout the week of the inauguration. Culturally it would have been normal to have had satanic/traditional rituals on the night before the public Christian inauguration. The normative behavior is to try to appease both the dark side and the Christian God.

Instead, with the support of my friend, this leader kept his integrity and conducted only the Christian inauguration ceremony. He stated that he wanted to be a different type of leader, one who was honest and kept his promises to the people. And he certainly made a good start.

Saul, however, did not. He knew it was wrong to consult the medium, because it was he who had outlawed them in accordance with God's laws. But that didn't impact his actions when he was afraid. When he was desperate, he did whatever he had to in order to get answers. For Saul, the end justified the means.

Isn't it interesting that those around Saul knew where to find a medium? And isn't it even more interesting that she did in fact have supernatural powers to help Saul? And isn't it even more interesting still that Samuel responded to her call?

Do we have any idea of the powers of the supernatural world? Do we have any concept of their reality? Do we have any appreciation for those powers—both God's and Satan's—in our daily lives? I wonder.

> The king said to her, "Don't be afraid. What do you see?"
>
> The woman said, "I see a ghostly figure coming up out of the earth."
>
> "What does he look like?" he asked.
>
> "An old man wearing a robe is coming up," she said.
>
> Then Saul knew it was Samuel, and he bowed down and prostrated himself with his face to the ground.
>
> Samuel said to Saul, "Why have you disturbed me by bringing me up?"
>
> "I am in great distress," Saul said. "The Philistines are fighting against me, and God has departed from me. He no longer answers me, either by prophets or by dreams. So I have called on you to tell me what to do."
>
> Samuel said, "Why do you consult me, now that the Lord has departed from you and become your enemy? The Lord has done what he predicted through me. The Lord has torn the kingdom out of your hands and given it to one of your neighbors—to David. Because you did not obey the Lord or carry out his fierce wrath against the Amalekites, the Lord has done this to you

today. The LORD will deliver both Israel and you into the hands of the Philistines, and tomorrow you and your sons will be with me. The LORD will also give the army of Israel into the hands of the Philistines."

Immediately Saul fell full length on the ground, filled with fear because of Samuel's words. (vv. 13–20)

What was the result of Saul's efforts to get information no matter how wrong the source? The only result was a confirmation that he would die in battle the next day. No comfort, no solution, only confirmation of his worst fears.

The result of compromising our integrity is never what we hoped for.

David's Integrity

David was exactly the same person whether in the fields tending sheep, in the battle fighting Goliath, in the palace as king, or anywhere else he happened to be. It seems to be one of the key characteristics of people after God's heart that they never feel the need to be someone other than just who they are.

Let's look at some opportunities that David had to take his destiny into his own hands and ensure his future. Let's see what he did consistently when the opportunities presented themselves. Let's begin with a chapter in David's life when he was on the run from Saul. He had already been anointed king by Samuel. He had already served Saul for many years but had to run from the palace under threat of death. Then together with the band of men we discussed earlier (the discontents, debtors, distressed, and refugees) he was hiding from Saul.

After Saul returned from pursuing the Philistines, he was told, "David is in the Desert of En Gedi." So Saul took three thousand able young men from all Israel and set out to look for David and his men near the Crags of the Wild Goats.

He came to the sheep pens along the way; a cave was there, and Saul went in to relieve himself. David and his men were far back in the cave. The men said, "This is the day the LORD spoke of when he said to you, 'I will give your enemy into your hands for you to deal with as you wish.'" Then David crept up unnoticed and cut off a corner of Saul's robe.

Afterward, David was conscience-stricken for having cut off a corner of his robe. He said to his men, "The LORD forbid that I should do such a thing to my master, the LORD's anointed, or lay my hand on him; for he is the anointed of the LORD." With these words David sharply rebuked his men and did not allow them to attack Saul. And Saul left the cave and went his way. (1 Samuel 24:1–7)

David was in the desert, hiding from Saul, and Saul came after him with three thousand men. Then in the same cave where David and his men were hiding, Saul chose to enter and use it as a toilet. David's men encouraged him to kill Saul and take over his inheritance. Instead, David, without being noticed, cut off a corner of Saul's robe. But even in this act, David's conscience told him this was wrong. So he stopped. How easy it would have been to justify killing Saul as God's will.

Even more amazing to me, he stopped his men from harming Saul. That was phenomenal leadership! They must have had tremendous respect for David. These were bandits, rough-and-ready, violent men on the run. They could have, in a single move, gone from being outlaws to inheriting the palace; but David stopped them by his word—and his example.

Have you ever known leaders like this? Ones who do not strive after power and position, but instead trust that if they are to move into such a position God will bring it about?

I do; in fact, I have several who work with me. It always amazes me that here are wonderfully qualified leaders of the first rank who could easily find a way to remove me from leadership if they chose to and take my job. But they consistently choose instead to follow my leadership and support it.

There are amazing lessons in "followership" in what David did here. And this was not a one-time event in David's life; he actually made it a habit. Let's move over to 1 Samuel 26 and watch him doing almost exactly the same thing again as Saul chased after him with three thousand men.

> Then David set out and went to the place where Saul had camped. He saw where Saul and Abner son of Ner, the commander of the army, had lain down. Saul was lying inside the camp, with the army encamped around him.
>
> . . . So David and Abishai went to the army by night, and there was Saul, lying asleep inside the camp with his spear stuck in the ground near his head. Abner and the soldiers were lying around him.
>
> Abishai said to David, "Today God has delivered your enemy into your hands. Now let me pin him to the ground with one thrust of the spear; I won't strike him twice."
>
> But David said to Abishai, "Don't destroy him! Who can lay a hand on the LORD's anointed and be guiltless? As surely as the LORD lives," he said, "the LORD himself will strike him, or his time will come and he will die, or he will go into battle and perish. But the LORD forbid that I should lay a hand on the LORD's anointed. Now get the spear and water jug that are near his head, and let's go."
>
> So David took the spear and water jug near Saul's head, and they left. No one saw or knew about it, nor

did anyone wake up. They were all sleeping, because the
Lord had put them into a deep sleep. (vv. 5–12)

David once again had the opportunity to grab his own destiny. Abishai offered to kill Saul for his leader and pointed out that this opportunity must be an act of God. But David declined, and instead he merely made his point, hoping that Saul would leave him alone if he realized that David was not a threat.

This truly was a lifelong habit of David's—to trust God with his life and role, rather than trying to control his own destiny. It happened again when Absalom, David's son, usurped the kingdom. As David and those loyal to him were fleeing Jerusalem, the priests picked up the ark of the covenant, the symbol of God's power and blessing, to bring it with them; but David stopped them: "Then the king said to Zadok, 'Take the ark of God back into the city. If I find favor in the Lord's eyes, he will bring me back and let me see it and his dwelling place again. But if he says, "I am not pleased with you," then I am ready; let him do to me whatever seems good to him'" (2 Samuel 15:25–26).

David once again refused to steal the symbol of God's presence and blessing and left it up to God to either return him to power or not.

David's integrity shone in another area consistently throughout his life. This was his response when one of his enemies died. I am not talking about the Philistines or God's enemies, but rather someone who held the power over David's position and future.

First, let's look at David's reaction when Saul died. Keep in mind that the death of this man opened the way for David to quit running and hiding in caves and the desert. The death of Saul enabled David to move into his inheritance as king over Israel. This was David's reaction when he heard of Saul's death:

> Then David said to the young man who brought him
> the report, "How do you know that Saul and his son
> Jonathan are dead?"

"I happened to be on Mount Gilboa," the young man said, "and there was Saul, leaning on his spear, with the chariots and their drivers in hot pursuit. When he turned around and saw me, he called out to me, and I said, 'What can I do?'

"He asked me, 'Who are you?'

"'An Amalekite,' I answered.

"Then he said to me, 'Stand here by me and kill me! I'm in the throes of death, but I'm still alive.'

"So I stood beside him and killed him, because I knew that after he had fallen he could not survive. And I took the crown that was on his head and the band on his arm and have brought them here to my lord."

Then David and all the men with him took hold of their clothes and tore them. They mourned and wept and fasted till evening for Saul and his son Jonathan, and for the army of the Lord and the house of Israel, because they had fallen by the sword.

David said to the young man who brought him the report, "Where are you from?"

"I am the son of a foreigner, an Amalekite," he answered.

David asked him, "Why weren't you afraid to lift your hand to destroy the Lord's anointed?"

Then David called one of his men and said, "Go, strike him down!" So he struck him down, and he died. (2 Samuel 1:5–15)

At first reading, we may be confused at David's response of executing the young man who brought him the news of Saul's death, but there was much more going on here. First of all, David was genuinely upset that Jonathan was dead as well as Saul. We will look more deeply into Jonathan and David's relationship in the next chapter.

For now, understand that David was deeply grieved over the news of Jonathan's death.

Second, this young man, even though a foreigner, knew that if Saul died, David was the next king. He was an opportunist and took it on himself to bring the new king what he logically thought would be good news. He thought he was in the right place at the right time and was looking for a reward from David. Instead, David saw through his evil motives and had him killed.

A few more years of war then followed between the house of Saul and the house of David, as Saul's former military chief set up Saul's son as king and waged war against David on his behalf. Then after a series of intrigues, love stories, and murders, someone murdered Saul's son and brought David his head. David's consistent integrity shone again in his response to those who murdered Ish-Bosheth.

> They brought the head of Ish-Bosheth to David at Hebron and said to the king, "Here is the head of Ish-Bosheth son of Saul, your enemy, who tried to take your life. This day the LORD has avenged my lord the king against Saul and his offspring."
>
> David answered Rekab and his brother Baanah, the sons of Rimmon the Beerothite, "As surely as the LORD lives, who has delivered me out of every trouble, when someone told me, 'Saul is dead,' and thought he was bringing good news, I seized him and put him to death in Ziklag. That was the reward I gave him for his news! How much more—when wicked men have killed an innocent man in his own house and on his own bed—should I not now demand his blood from your hand and rid the earth of you!" (2 Samuel 4:8–11)

Here again David's response was not one of joy over the death of his enemy, even though it removed the obstruction for him to rule over the entire nation of Israel. Rather David is horrified over the fact that they murdered an innocent man.

And a third time David heard of the death of an enemy was when Absalom, David's son who stole the kingdom from him, was killed in battle. David found no joy in the news, even though it meant his kingdom would be restored to him: "The king was shaken. He went up to the room over the gateway and wept. As he went, he said: 'O my son Absalom! My son, my son Absalom! If only I had died instead of you—O Absalom, my son, my son!'" (2 Samuel 18:33).

How do we measure up to David's standard of integrity? Do we mourn and weep when our competitors fail? How about the opposite? Are we able to rejoice when a church down the street grows? How about when another ministry flourishes financially while we are struggling in that area? Do we rejoice with them, or do we secretly wish they would fail, thinking that somehow that would make us look better?

I know about one situation where competitors in ministry (and, yes, these were all Christian leaders) had fellow ministers of the gospel arrested on false charges, just to stop their ministry from thriving. In a country where persecution is frequent and harsh, a man went to the police and made false claims against other church planters with the express goal of getting them arrested so that his ministry would thrive and theirs would decline.

That may be the extreme case, but jealousy is a strong motivator. It causes us at times to do ridiculous things or at least contemplate them. Maybe we would never do anything evil to another ministry or Christian leader, but would we want to?

Saul was willing to do anything necessary to stay in power, whether it was to kill God's anointed next leader or consult a demonic spiritist. He had no problem doing whatever he thought might work in order to protect his throne and himself.

David, on the other hand, refused to take advantage of any situation that would give him more power or solve his problems at the cost of harming others. He refused to compromise to protect his position and his throne. In fact, he genuinely mourned over his enemies when they died and honored them publicly instead.

Do your private life and your public actions match? That is the definition of integrity. Are you the same person whether people are watching or not?

Does your leadership look more like Saul's or David's?

Questions for Reflection:

- Does your public image match your private life?
- Have you ever sought and followed counsel that lacked integrity?
- What are your honest reactions when a competitor in ministry fails? Compare your reactions with David's when his enemies died.

QUESTION 5:
Do I Let People Get Close Enough to Really Love Me?

"Just remember now," the speaker continued, "one of your responsibilities as a pastor and a leader is to never let anyone get too close to you. The problem is that if people see you for who you really are they will be disappointed. You need to have a certain image as a Christian leader. You cannot let that image be tarnished. And if people get too close—well, you can just imagine what would happen."

Does that sound like fiction to you? Or does it sound familiar? There are seminaries that teach exactly this line of reasoning even today. They teach that you should stay at arm's length from those you lead so that they will respect you.

What a tragedy! What a ridiculous and ungodly notion, because in fact exactly the opposite is true. As a leader you need friendships to sustain you. You need those you can rely on, who will support you in the worst of times as well as the best of times.

The image of the macho loner who can take on the world is a Western creation. The "Marlboro man" billboards capture it perfectly. This is the billboard image of the cowboy sitting alone, looking out over the range that is his kingdom. He appears to be totally self-sustained, taking a long draw on his Marlboro cigarette.

That concept of leadership is as false as the concept that to be "cool" you need to smoke cigarettes. Cigarettes will kill you eventually and so will trying to go it alone as a leader.

Saul's Close Relationships

If we look carefully at Saul's life, we have no record of close relationships, of those who loved him and walked with him purely because of their deep respect. It is curious in a way because there are characters in his story who follow him all of their lives. Two who come to mind are Abner, who headed his army, and Jonathan his son. But there is nothing in the biblical accounts that tell us of deep and passionate bonds of friendship between Saul and those who served him. Probably the closest relationship that we know about was between Samuel and Saul. Most of what we know about that relationship is that Samuel grieved over Saul and his failures.

David's Close Relationships

David's story, in comparison, is rich with deep relationships. David had a wonderfully loyal following of those who held him very dear. I think it would have been easy to like David and easy to be his friend. He obviously let people get close to him and treasured relationships.

Certainly it is never very easy to tell who your friends are when you are the king, the president, or hold any position of power. Generally speaking, there are lots of people happy to be your friend at that point.

It is much easier to tell who your real friends are when things are going badly. At times when you lose your job, your position of power, or your throne, then it is a little clearer who are your real friends. Let's look at three examples of those who loved David so much that they were willing to lose their positions of power or even die for him.

The Three Mighty Warriors

Let's start with "the three mighty warriors." We get their description in 2 Samuel 23 in the middle of the description of David's mighty men. Let's see what their devotion to David looked like.

> During harvest time, three of the thirty chief warriors came down to David at the cave of Adullam, while a band of Philistines was encamped in the Valley of Rephaim. At that time David was in the stronghold, and the Philistine garrison was at Bethlehem. David longed for water and said, "Oh, that someone would get me a drink of water from the well near the gate of Bethlehem!" So the three mighty warriors broke through the Philistine lines, drew water from the well near the gate of Bethlehem and carried it back to David. But he refused to drink it; instead, he poured it out before the LORD. "Far be it from me, LORD, to do this!" he said. "Is it not the blood of men who went at the risk of their lives?" And David would not drink it.
>
> Such were the exploits of the three mighty warriors.
> (vv. 13–17)

David was trapped at the stronghold by the Philistines. He was not in a position of power or success at this point. These three mighty warriors came to him, and he expressed a desire for a drink of water from the well at Bethlehem. Yes, he may have been thirsty; but the deep desire for water from that particular well speaks of his desire to see the land rid of the Philistines and his promise of kingship fulfilled. It had been a long, hard fight, and he was still on the run. He was probably tired and discouraged, and he was being emotionally vulnerable.

David was expressing a deep longing. He was sharing his feelings with those around him and not expecting anyone to act on that expression. But these three mighty men were so dedicated to him that they braved impossible odds just to fulfill his deepest desire. They wanted to encourage David and show him their dedication and their assurance that whatever he wished, no matter how dangerous, they would make it happen.

Somehow they got through the Philistine battle lines, drew water from the well, and carried it back through the Philistine lines to David. This was an act of bravado, yes, but more than that, it was an act of love and dedication.

David's response is quite interesting as well. Can you imagine the scene as the three warriors arrive, breathless, with dust caked on their sweating brows. I wonder if any of them was slightly wounded and bleeding.

David was overwhelmed, and there must have been tears of deep gratitude in his eyes. But even here he was thinking first of God. He realized he could not drink this water because it was too precious. He realized that what had been given to him had become sacred water.

He took the cup in both hands, offered a prayer of gratitude for men of such valor around him, and then he poured out the water with reverence as a drink offering before the Lord. He did this because he realized this was a sacred act of love and dedication that these men had undertaken. To have kept it for himself would have been cheapening their sacrifice. By giving it to the Lord, he let his men know that, though they did it for him, it was really an act of worship for God.

These were not boys out foolishly risking their lives to prove something. These were seasoned warriors who counted the cost but wanted so badly to show their love and commitment to their leader that they risked their lives to fulfill his desire.

Would those who work for you do something similar? Do they love and respect you enough to risk everything for you? People take risks of this type only for those they completely trust, for those they care for very deeply, and for those they have been loved by.

His Wife Michal

Michal was David's first love and his first wife. Their love story has several fascinating pieces, but none of them were simple. Michal was of course the daughter of Saul, which made their relationship inherently fraught with challenges. Saul was not only the king trying to kill David but also his father-in-law.

We know that there was from the beginning a special attraction between Michal and David, because Saul tried to get David to marry Michal's older sister, Merab. David, however, politely refused. But as it came time for Michal to marry, David reacted differently.

When Saul realized that David and Michal loved each other, he used that knowledge to try to trap David. He required David to pay a bride price for Michal of one hundred Philistine foreskins. Saul hoped David would be so driven by his love that he would attempt the nearly impossible challenge and get killed in the process. (And you thought your father-in-law was difficult.) David succeeded in accomplishing that feat and so married the king's daughter.

When David had to flee for his life, Saul gave Michal to another husband, whom she was married to for many years. But at the very first opportunity, David asked for her to return. He asked for her as the first token of peace from Abner, the head of Saul's army, and Ish-Bosheth, Saul's son who was then the acting king. This was after Saul's death, though before peace was established between the house of Saul and the house of David. We do not know all of David's motivations for that act, but it may have simply been that he deeply missed her.

We do have one story that tells us of Michal's deep love and devotion for David. The setting is when David was still serving as a part of Saul's household, but it was becoming clear that Saul definitely planned to kill him. David realized he must escape but first went home to Michal.

> Saul sent men to David's house to watch it and to kill him in the morning. But Michal, David's wife, warned him, "If you don't run for your life tonight, tomorrow you'll be killed." So Michal let David down through a window, and he fled and escaped. Then Michal took an idol and laid it on the bed, covering it with a garment and putting some goats' hair at the head.
>
> When Saul sent the men to capture David, Michal said, "He is ill."
>
> Then Saul sent the men back to see David and told them, "Bring him up to me in his bed so that I may kill him." But when the men entered, there was the idol in the bed, and at the head was some goats' hair.
>
> Saul said to Michal, "Why did you deceive me like this and send my enemy away so that he escaped?"
>
> Michal told him, "He said to me, 'Let me get away. Why should I kill you?'" (1 Samuel 19:11–17)

Michal took David's side against her father, warned him to flee, enabled him to do so, and then created an elaborate diversion to give him plenty of time to get away. This was quite a brave act. And Michal then told her father a plausible lie when some of her actions became known.

Whatever else may or may not have been ideal in the relationship from our perspective, it is clear that Michal genuinely loved David and happily risked her own life for him against her own family.

David was deeply loved by those close to him. He loved Michal and took significant risks to marry her and later to get her back. She responded to that love and returned it at great personal risk.

Jonathan

I have saved for last the story of David and Jonathan's friendship. Jonathan was the best and most famous of David's close friends. He was Saul's oldest son and therefore heir to the throne. We do not know exactly when David and Jonathan met, but we do know when their friendship was solidified. It was right after David killed Goliath.

> As soon as David returned from killing the Philistine, Abner took him and brought him before Saul, with David still holding the Philistine's head.
>
> "Whose son are you, young man?" Saul asked him.
>
> David said, "I am the son of your servant Jesse of Bethlehem."
>
> After David had finished talking with Saul, Jonathan became one in spirit with David, and he loved him as himself. From that day Saul kept David with him and did not let him return home to his family. And Jonathan made a covenant with David because he loved him as himself. Jonathan took off the robe he was wearing and gave it to David, along with his tunic, and even his sword, his bow and his belt. (1 Samuel 17:57–18:4)

We do not have a lot of description about why Jonathan loved David, but it is clear that he did. We do know that David and Jonathan were both mighty warriors, which probably created a bond of mutual respect between them. Jonathan was also a truly good man and just as consistent as David in his character. He was deeply loyal, upright, and brave. We can see it in his treatment of David as well as in the stories of the battles he fought.

Meanwhile, Saul's feelings toward David turned from admiration to distrust and jealousy. That jealousy just kept escalating as Saul realized that God was with David, that his daughter Michal loved him, and that David was growing in fame due to his success in battle.

In fact, Saul finally grew so jealous that he told Jonathan and all the attendants to kill David. But Jonathan warned David so he could hide. What is fascinating though is that Jonathan went even further than that. He took his father aside in an attempt to reconcile him and David, which worked—temporarily.

> Jonathan spoke well of David to Saul his father and said to him, "Let not the king do wrong to his servant David; he has not wronged you, and what he has done has benefited you greatly. He took his life in his hands when he killed the Philistine. The LORD won a great victory for all Israel, and you saw it and were glad. Why then would you do wrong to an innocent man like David by killing him for no reason?"
>
> Saul listened to Jonathan and took this oath: "As surely as the LORD lives, David will not be put to death."
>
> So Jonathan called David and told him the whole conversation. He brought him to Saul, and David was with Saul as before. (1 Samuel 19:4–7)

Jonathan acted here as the peacemaker. He persuaded his father to be reasonable and realize that David was not an enemy. And wonderfully Saul listened to him and responded well.

Here was another of Saul's children who took David's side against his own father. Jonathan was acting as an honest reconciler, trying to bring his father and his best friend together because he believed it would be in everyone's best interest and because he loved them both.

But then Saul's anger and jealousy flared again at David, and David and Jonathan talked over what to do. Let's take a look at one part of that meeting.

Then Jonathan said to David, "I swear by the Lord, the God of Israel, that I will surely sound out my father by this time the day after tomorrow! If he is favorably disposed toward you, will I not send you word and let you know? But if my father intends to harm you, may the Lord deal with me, be it ever so severely, if I do not let you know and send you away in peace. May the Lord be with you as he has been with my father. But show me unfailing kindness like the Lord's kindness as long as I live, so that I may not be killed, and do not ever cut off your kindness from my family—not even when the Lord has cut off every one of David's enemies from the face of the earth."

So Jonathan made a covenant with the house of David, saying, "May the Lord call David's enemies to account." And Jonathan had David reaffirm his oath out of love for him, because he loved him as he loved himself. (1 Samuel 20:12–17)

Jonathan swore to warn David of whatever Saul planned to do. And he also seems to have clearly understood that David was God's choice for the throne in the future. He gave David a very specific blessing: "May the Lord be with you as he has been with my father." How much clearer could Jonathan have made it?

Then Jonathan renewed his covenant with David and reaffirmed his love for him. As the Bible puts it, Jonathan loved David "as he loved himself."

Actually it seems that he loved David more than he loved himself. Saul pointed this out in frustration when Jonathan was trying to defend David's failure to show up at a feast. Listen to Saul's words:

Saul's anger flared up at Jonathan and he said to him, "You son of a perverse and rebellious woman! Don't I know that you have sided with the son of Jesse to your own shame and to the shame of the mother who bore you? As long as the son of Jesse lives on this earth, neither you nor your kingdom will be established. Now send someone to bring him to me, for he must die!"

"Why should he be put to death? What has he done?" Jonathan asked his father. But Saul hurled his spear at him to kill him. Then Jonathan knew that his father intended to kill David.

Jonathan got up from the table in fierce anger; on that second day of the feast he did not eat, because he was grieved at his father's shameful treatment of David. (1 Samuel 20:30–34)

Saul was angry at Jonathan for taking David's side. He yelled at him that he was throwing away his future as well as the whole family's legacy by taking David's side. You can imagine the frustration in Saul's voice. Then Saul hurled a spear at his own son, and Jonathan walked away angry and grieved.

This was a violent argument between father and son. They both saw the reality—that David would be king and take over the throne—but responded to that outcome completely differently. Saul saw it as an unnecessary threat and tragedy. Jonathan saw it through God's eyes of love for David.

What is probably most amazing here is that Jonathan was not at all troubled about the fact that David would get the power and glory of the throne instead of him. He seems to have been totally at peace about that and had no shred of jealousy. He truly loved David more than himself!

Then Jonathan went to the appointed meeting place and signaled David through the boy with the arrows about the outcome of the meeting with his father. After sending the boy away, Jonathan and David wept, embraced, and kissed. This was surely their last meeting together, and at some level they seem to have instinctively realized this.

From there David went into hiding and was on the run until Saul's death. Meanwhile, Jonathan went back to serve his father and fulfill his duties to him. The deep bond of friendship that supersedes family, wealth, and position was the bond of friendship that David and Jonathan enjoyed.

David's lament for Jonathan when he hears of his death is one of those beautiful pieces of poetry about true friendship and brotherhood.

> How the mighty have fallen in battle!
> Jonathan lies slain on your heights.
> I grieve for you, Jonathan my brother;
> you were very dear to me.
> Your love for me was wonderful,
> more wonderful than that of women.
> (2 Samuel 1:25–26)

Many of us are born with brothers and sisters we dearly love, but those we choose as our friends often become just as precious, if not more. Those friendships at their best reflect God's love for us as we share our lives with each other, both the good times and the deepest difficulties.

I had the rare privilege once of spending an evening with a group of leaders of a denomination in East Africa who had some of the most precious friendships with each other that I have ever observed in a leadership team.

I was the guest of one of these leaders, Nicholas Wafula, and his wife, Elisabeth, who were having a group of close friends over for dinner one night. These friends had worked together, worshiped together, and raised their families together over thirty years of ministry growing the Deliverance Church. They had also suffered together under the horrors of the evil regime of Idi Amin.

I truly do not think I have ever laughed as hard as I did that night as they told stories of recent events as well as those that happened long ago. But I also cried with them as they told recent stories of painful losses. Then they invited me to join them in worship and pray with them as they talked of the Lord's goodness, his faithfulness, and his love.

The gentle respect these men and women had for each other was lovely. The humility each had, the way they loved one another more than position or power, the deep caring that was expressed—all of this spoke of thirty years of growing together and caring for one another. I went to sleep that night thinking that this is the way the body of Christ is supposed to look. This is the way we should love one another.

There are many more stories of those who served David out of deep respect and love. Leaders who love and serve those they lead engender those kinds of emotions in others. If you want to know how to earn the love of those you work with, it is really quite simple. Love them first. It is what God did with us.

We were made for deep and lasting friendships with each other and with God. We need those kinds of deep and lasting friendships. We need them when we go through the deepest valleys of pain and disappointment and failure in this world. And we need them to celebrate when good things happen in our lives.

How do those who work for you feel about you? Do they hold a deep respect and even love for you? Or do they tolerate you or work for you out of fear of losing their jobs or worse? Does your leadership look more like Saul's or David's?

Questions for Reflection:

- Does your pride stop you from letting people see your faults and your vulnerabilities?
- Do you let people get to know you well enough to actually love you for who you really are?
- Are you willing to be dependent on others? Do you have friends who can provide the encouragement and protection you need?

Do I Lead from the Security of Knowing God's Love?

As we come to the close of this book, there is one more question you need to ask yourself, though it is not one of the five questions about symptoms of our leadership that we have been asking. This is the core question that makes or breaks everything.

The question is, Do I lead from the security of knowing God's love? And no matter how you answer that question, the next one you must ask is, How do I learn to let God love me more?

We must have the security of resting in God's love in order to lead successfully from God's perspective. It is not optional. It is foundational. And no matter how much of that is in your life, there is more available. Growing in your ability to let God love you and loving him in return are an endless and marvelous adventure. It is what this life is really supposed to be all about.

If you are a believer, you know that God loves you and that God is love. Those are the facts on which our faith is built. Yet one of the most pivotal questions that you may ever ask yourself is whether that influences how you lead.

Do you lead out of the security of knowing and believing God loves you? Do you believe that it is impossible to earn his love or to deserve his love? Do you know that he loves you in the same way a mother loves her child, deeply, instinctively, and no matter what you do?

Or do you lead hoping that you may somehow earn God's love through the outcomes of your work? Do you believe that God is a demanding, jealous, and zealous God and that you must be successful in all the work he has called you to do so that he will then love you?

That is bad theology from beginning to end. So, if it is impossible to earn God's love, let me ask you honestly, Why are you still trying so hard? Why are you so busy? Why are you so tired and worn out? Why do you continually find yourself on the edge of burnout, trying to cope with the load that is too heavy for you to carry?

While there are many complex reasons that contribute to those ills, at the very core of all of them is the need for a deeper understanding of God's unfailing love for us. The truth is that there is absolutely nothing you can do to cause God not to love you and that there is absolutely nothing you can do to earn more of God's love.

All that he wants us to do is grow in our acceptance and understanding of his love for us and respond appropriately. When our leadership is based on the security of being loved, almost everything else comes into proper perspective. Competition fades away because we do not need to compete. Jealousy, strife, and anger cease. Fear, with its ugly tentacles gripping our heart of hearts, dissolves as perfect love casts out fear.

Saul unfortunately never understood this, but David did. Consistently and regularly the difference—the only difference—between Saul and David's leadership was the heart.

We never get any sense that Saul loved God or understood God's love for him. We have no story or memory recorded that indicates that Saul's security was in his acceptance and understanding of God's love for him. In fact, there is evidence to the contrary.

Saul did not honor God, as we see from his repeated disobedience to God's commands in order to get what he wanted. He feared the opinions of others, as he regularly gave in to his men rather than risk losing their favor. He feared the loss of power as jealousy grew in his heart, watching David's successes in battle and resulting growth of reputation.

One fascinating revelation of Saul's heart is his visit to the witch in Endor, which we talked about in chapter 6. Oddly enough, he trusted Samuel and his words more than he trusted God. See how misplaced his faith was? Rather than trusting in the God whom Samuel served, he violated God's laws in order to have Samuel brought back from the dead to tell him what to do and console him. And of course his efforts failed to bring him any comfort. Samuel only repeated what he had already told Saul—that he would die the next day.

Saul was God's chosen leader, anointed by God, called by God, and filled with God's Spirit—and yet he did not love God or let God love him. His failure was a failure of the heart: "Saul died because he was unfaithful to the LORD; he did not keep the word of the LORD and even consulted a medium for guidance, and did not inquire of the LORD. So the LORD put him to death and turned the kingdom over to David son of Jesse" (1 Chronicles 10:13–14).

The comparison to David could not be more extreme in this one area. Yes, David was called, anointed, and filled with God's Spirit. David even sinned in significant ways just like Saul. But what is different between these two men at the very core is that David loved God with all of his heart. He loved God in response to God's love. David let God love him, and David loved God in return.

Throughout the stories of David's life this is the consistent theme, and it matures, ripens, and becomes more lovely as David's life progresses. Psalm 51 is one of the beautiful love songs of David to God.

> Have mercy on me, O God,
>> according to your unfailing love;
> according to your great compassion
>> blot out my transgressions.
> Wash away all my iniquity
>> and cleanse me from my sin.
> . . . Cleanse me with hyssop, and I will be clean;
>> wash me, and I will be whiter than snow.
> . . . Create in me a pure heart, O God,
>> and renew a steadfast spirit within me.
> Do not cast me from your presence
>> or take your Holy Spirit from me.
> Restore to me the joy of your salvation
>> and grant me a willing spirit, to sustain me.
> . . . Open my lips, Lord,
>> and my mouth will declare your praise.
> You do not delight in sacrifice, or I would bring it;
>> you do not take pleasure in burnt offerings.
> My sacrifice, O God, is a broken spirit;
>> a broken and contrite heart
>> you, God, will not despise. (excerpts from Psalm 51)

And again in Psalm 63:1–8 we get a glimpse of the passionate love relationship David had with God.

> You, God, are my God,
>> earnestly I seek you;
> I thirst for you,
>> my whole being longs for you,
> in a dry and parched land
>> where there is no water.
> I have seen you in the sanctuary

and beheld your power and your glory.
Because your love is better than life,
    my lips will glorify you.
I will praise you as long as I live,
    and in your name I will lift up my hands.
I will be fully satisfied as with the richest of foods;
    with singing lips my mouth will praise you.
On my bed I remember you;
    I think of you through the watches of the night.
Because you are my help,
    I sing in the shadow of your wings.
I cling to you;
    your right hand upholds me.

"Your love is better than life" (v. 3). David did not fear death because he had tasted the love of God. He had lived in God's love. It mattered more to him than anything else.

God's promise to David regarding his descendants and his kingdom was a loving encouragement to him:

> The LORD declares to you that the LORD himself will establish a house for you: When your days are over and you rest with your ancestors, I will raise up your offspring to succeed you, who will come from your own body, and I will establish his kingdom. He is the one who will build a house for my Name, and I will establish the throne of his kingdom forever. I will be his father, and he will be my son. When he does wrong, I will punish him with a rod wielded by human beings, with floggings inflicted by human hands. But my love will never be taken away from him, as I took it away from Saul, whom I removed from before you. Your house and your kingdom will endure forever before me; your throne will be established forever. (2 Samuel 7:11–16)

God answered the deepest question of David's heart in this passage. In verse 15 he promised David, "My love will never be taken away from him, as I took it away from Saul." God knew that in David's heart there was a question of losing God's love and favor through sin.

God's promise was clear to David. God knew the future, and he knew that he would never stop loving David's offspring. Ultimately Jesus would come from David's descendants, and we who are believers in Jesus today inherit the blessing God promised to David.

Saul would not let God love him. He would not accept God's love and turned his heart away. God will not force us to love him because love is a description of a relationship, an emotion, and a choice of the will.

David was in love with God, and it was that love that fueled his life and leadership. Even when he failed, he repented and turned back to God and asked God to cleanse his heart. He trusted God deeply with his whole life—his present circumstances and his entire future.

Letting God Love You

The key here is letting God love you and then responding to that love. I used to think that loving God was the key, and it seemed to me to be just one more difficult discipline, one more rule in the Christian faith. To me it was the hardest rule: Love the Lord your God with all your heart, with all your soul, and with all your strength. Yet how do you make yourself love someone?

You can make yourself get along with someone. You can make yourself respect and accept someone. You can make yourself do a lot of things. But loving is an act of the heart, and the only way to love is to be loved. We love God because he first loved us. You must open your heart to God and let him love you first.

Learning to let God love me has been a lifelong undertaking, but what a glorious one. I want to share with you one of my most recent experiences of this journey, because it was so surprising to me and so refreshing at the same time. Letting God love you is such a personal thing, that I have to share with you one of my experiences of this, because I do not know exactly how it looks to anyone else. I cannot tell their story.

It all began when the board of directors of the ministry I lead could see that I was in need of a break. They asked me to take a sabbatical of one to three months, and I chose one month. I just could not believe that I should take more time than that away from work. (Yes, I am a driven, performance-based personality.)

Because of the urging of my prayer partners and the voice of the Holy Spirit, I took one week of that time to escape to a cabin in the mountains to be alone with God. My sense was that he had something important he wanted to say to me. I was wondering if this would include direction for the ministry I lead, a change of direction for my own future, or instructions of some type. I had no real clue, but I knew it was important.

From the time I started my journey to the cabin, and then continuing throughout that entire week alone there, do you know what God did? He told me how much he loves me.

That was it—but, oh my, what an amazing and wonderful time it was! I wish I could explain it or describe it or somehow take you there with me, but most of all I just want you to long for that same kind of experience. At the end of the week, I found myself begging God, "Please don't make me go back. Please, can I just go to be with you now? I never, ever want to stop feeling what I am feeling right now."

Nothing has ever been quite the same since then. I just cannot be as upset about the everyday challenges. I cannot get quite as frustrated when things go wrong or people around me fail or I fail those around me. I cannot get quite as fearful over the daily news of wars and rumors of wars. I just cannot care quite as much about this world as I did before, but I do seem to love those in it more.

And isn't that exactly the fruit he promises for those who walk with him? Perfect love does cast out fear. Seeing the world from God's loving perspective changes how I see everything. Truly everything is different.

I still work too hard sometimes, but then I also catch myself more quickly and remember what really matters. I still fail, get frustrated and fearful, but those times are shorter and less devastating.

True leadership must be based in the security of God's love. It establishes different marks of success than leadership based on fear. You then lead to please God and to bring him joy. Everything is viewed through the perspective of God's kingdom values, and therefore it does not quite fit the perspective of this world.

As long as we are working so hard at being self-sufficient, self-disciplined, and self-_____ (you fill in the blank), we are missing the most important part. We love God because he first loved us. The most important task of leadership is to let God love us and to respond to that love. From that place of security, of deep and quiet fulfillment and rightly placed priorities, flows godly leadership. It becomes a natural outflowing of our lives.

That is all God asks—that we let him love us, which, in turn, makes us love him.

How to Let God Love You

I have no new truth for you on this subject of how to let God love you, but there are some biblical means that are dramatically simple. And yet we all struggle so hard to live them.

In order to be a successful leader you have to lead from the secure place of knowing God loves you. In order to find that resting place, you simply need to do the following:

1. Spend time alone with God daily.
2. Practice the spiritual disciplines.
3. Regularly celebrate and rest with those you love.

As we look at each of these means, ask God to show you how to grow in each area.

Spend Time Alone with God Daily

There is no possibility of having a relationship with someone unless you spend time with that person. Today's technology allows you more and more options for developing relationships. You can build connections on Facebook, on Skype, in a restaurant, or walking beside a river; but whatever medium you choose, it still requires contact, effort, focus, and time.

Similarly, there are innumerable ways to spend time with God. There is no perfect formula for how to do this, what to do, or when to do it. Ask God for guidance, and utilize any and all resources you find helpful.

The real key is simply doing it—making it a priority to get alone with God. It is impossible to let God love you unless you spend time with him. And we humans are so easily distracted by worldly concerns that seem to crowd in on us. We need to increase our attention span when we turn our focus to eternal matters. Drawing away from the frantic world and into the sweet presence of God is essential for our physical and spiritual health.

"Seek first his kingdom . . . and all these things will be given to you as well." That is a principle that God has made clear to me, telling me to make it the first thing that I do every day. There are lovely phrases in the Psalms and in Isaiah about seeking God in the morning, though admittedly this may just be a personal preference of mine.

What I am sure about is that a leader has to spend time alone with God daily. Seek his face; talk with him; listen to him; do this in whatever way works best for you. But the critical key is much like the Nike commercial says, "Just do it," and the rewards will be utterly amazing.

Practice the Spiritual Disciplines

If you do not know what I mean by "spiritual disciplines," then you need to find good resources to study this subject. Fortunately we are not alone in this quest for relationship with God. Many have gone before us and have left us with wonderful keys about how to know God better.

Prayer, fasting, solitude, Bible study, worship, and tithing are some of the ways that many heroes of the faith and the early church fathers were able to grow in their understanding of and relationship with God. We do not need to reinvent the wheel here. Have the humility to read and study what others have learned, and build on their experiences. Read broadly and deeply on these subjects, and let God teach you more about how others have successfully pursued him.

He desires intimacy with you. He is a God who loves to communicate. Give him the opportunity to mold and shape your life through practicing the disciplines of the faith. Broaden your experience by looking into spiritual disciplines that you have not practiced faithfully before. Don't limit yourself to the ones that appeal to you the most.

Regularly Celebrate and Rest with Those You Love

Find balance in your life through celebrating God's blessings and taking regular times of rest with those you love. This particular admonition is one aimed primarily at leaders. For some reason we are particularly adverse to relaxing and celebrating.

We even find theological reasons for this. I will never forget an Indian leader whom I love dearly saying to me with great seriousness, "Jane, I cannot take a vacation because every day thousands of people will die in this country without knowing about Jesus. How can I take a day off when that is happening?" He went on to explain that rather than celebrating Christmas with time off, he expected his staff to hold evangelistic campaigns away from their families.

Do you see the problem? It is impossible to please God in a state of exhaustion, hurting those closest to you. God designed us to need rest. Arguably, even God took a Sabbath after creating the world. Why would we think we do not need to rest? Why would we think God does not desire to give us rest?

Some of the most beautiful promises in the Bible are about giving us rest. It is during those times of rest and celebration that God often feeds our souls. He reminds us of his goodness to us. He draws those he has given us here on earth closer to us and teaches us about his love through our relationships with them. He nurtures us.

To fail to take the time to celebrate and rest with those we love cuts us off from being able to receive God's love. It severs our lifeline, just as surely as cutting the garden hose would deprive a tree of water necessary for its life. Without regular breaks we will shrivel up and lose perspective.

Our Creator has made this abundantly clear to us in his commands about Sabbath rest. To defy that is to once again assert our independence from him and go our own way, turning from his efforts to love us. It is impossible to please God and ignore his wisdom.

So just three simple things, right? Yet why are truly simple things so hard to do? It is because we are in a daily spiritual battle against our own flesh and against evil forces in the world. We can't ignore the spiritual weapons at our disposal for months on end, or even weeks, and think we can thrive in ministry. We truly will not even survive. We will fail. We will fall apart, and we will make God sorry he chose us for leadership.

But the opposite is also wonderfully true. If you choose daily to follow God with all of your heart and demonstrate that by following these three steps, I can guarantee that you will succeed. You will bring joy to God's heart. Pause and think of this privilege for a moment. Isn't that the most wonderful and exciting goal you can imagine? We can give back to God something he wants.

And that is exactly God's description of David's leadership. David was a man after his own heart. And that is exactly what he desires for you. That is why he has you here on earth—to be able to love you, so that you can love him and others in return and bring him glory and joy.

Take the simple steps. Let your life and leadership look more like David's than Saul's. The world may not notice, but God will. And he will use you to expand his kingdom on earth.

Questions for Reflection:

- Are you willing to stop being rebellious and learn to be dependent on God?
- Is your leadership grounded in the security of knowing God's love?
- Are you willing to take the time needed to find better ways of letting God love you?
- Will you start today?

Appendix

Defining Leadership Development—2008

Administered by Development Associates International

Q1. Think of the best experience you have had working under someone, in other words your best experience being led. (Check up to three characteristics below that best describe what made this person such a good leader for you.)

Answer Options	Response Percent	English Responses	Spanish Responses	Portugese Responses	Chinese Responses	French Responses
Integrity, authenticity, excellent character	69.4%	564	57	1	10	36
Servant's heart, humble	48.1%	391	46	1	5	56
Biblical knowledge, theologically sound	27.2%	221	33	0	5	19
Decisive, strong, and directive	12.4%	101	9	0	1	8
Compassionate, good listener, more oriented to people than accomplishing the task	26.6%	216	20	1	1	30
Compelling/charisma, visionary	12.8%	104	13	1	2	30
Excellent people management skills and ability to discern and develop the gifts of others	38.1%	310	23	0	0	43
Spiritually mature, hears God's voice, holy and prayerful	47.7%	388	39	1	5	30
Good communicator, teacher	17.7%	144	19	1	0	30
Other (please specify)	4.3%	35	8	0	0	5
answered question		813	85	2	10	94
skipped question		17	2	0	2	7

Q2. Think of the worst experience you have had working under someone, in other words your worst experience being led. (Check up to three characteristics below that best describe what made this person such a poor leader.)

Answer Options	Response Percent	English Responses	Spanish Responses	Portugese Responses	Chinese Responses	French Responses
Lack of integrity, untrustworthy	48.9%	387	48	1	8	34
Prideful, always right, and always the big boss	61.7%	488	62	1	3	67
Theologically unsound, lack of biblical knowledge	12.1%	96	15	0	1	5
Indecisive, weak	19.6%	155	11	0	3	9
Harsh, uncaring, refused to listen, critical	42.9%	339	40	1	1	53
Lack of vision or ability to influence others	24.1%	191	12	1	4	7
Inability to manage people and enable them to work together	32.4%	256	16	1	2	28
Spiritually immature, no evidence of holiness or prayerfulness	22.6%	179	25	0	3	20
Inability to communicate or teach	15.7%	124	10	1	4	18
Other (please specify)	10.2%	81	9	0	0	8
	answered question	791	85	2	10	90
	skipped question	39	2	0	2	11

Q3. Which of these qualities would you agree are most important to the success of a Christ-centered leader? (Check your top three from the list below.)

Answer Options	Response Percent	English Responses	Spanish Responses	Portugese Responses	Chinese Responses	French Responses
Integrity, authenticity, excellent character	72.2%	573	51	2	8	57
Servant's heart, humble	58.6%	465	52	1	4	54
Biblical knowledge, theologically sound	33.5%	266	39	1	5	13
Decisive, strong, and directive	5.5%	44	4	0	1	1
Compassionate, good listener, more oriented to people than accomplishing the task	24.4%	194	24	0	1	23
Compelling/charisma, visionary	9.4%	75	11	0	4	27
Excellent people management skills and ability to discern and develop the gifts of others	35.8%	284	23	1	1	46
Spiritually mature, hears God's voice, holy and prayerful	56.7%	450	51	1	5	39
Good communicator, teacher	11.2%	89	13	0	0	22
Comments		27	4	0	0	3
answered question		794	86	2	10	89
skipped question		36	1	0	2	12

Q4. Think of an example that you know of a really good leader who is not a Christian. Now think of an example of a really good leader who is a Christian. Are there any qualities present in the Christian leader that are missing from the non-Christian leader? (Do not do this "in theory," but think about real leaders you know. Check any qualities below that the Christian leader has that the non-Christian leader is missing that make a difference in their leadership.)

Answer Options	Response Percent	English Responses	Spanish Responses	Portugese Responses	Chinese Responses	French Responses
Integrity, authenticity, excellent character	24.9%	183	33	0	5	31
Servant's heart, humble	47.0%	345	48	0	8	51
Biblical knowledge, theologically sound	61.2%	449	68	2	6	48
Decisive, strong, and directive	4.0%	29	0	0	0	3
Compassionate, good listener, more oriented to people than accomplishing the task	16.9%	124	24	0	1	28
Compelling/charisma, visionary	4.2%	31	7	0	0	10
Excellent people management skills and ability to discern and develop the gifts of others	9.8%	72	15	1	0	22
Spiritually mature, hears God's voice, holy and prayerful	78.2%	574	64	2	7	61
Good communicator, teacher	6.5%	48	20	0	1	19
Comments		73	7	0	10	39
answered question		734	83	2	10	86
skipped question		96	4	0	2	15

Q5. If you could choose a simple phrase that most appropriately summed up Christ-centered leadership, what would you say?

Answer Options	Response Percent	English Responses	Spanish Responses	Portugese Responses	Chinese Responses	French Responses
answered question		703	82	2	7	86
skipped question		127	5	0	5	15

Q6. What is something you see Christian leaders doing often that they would not do if they were truly Christlike?

Answer Options	Response Percent	English Responses	Spanish Responses	Portugese Responses	Chinese Responses	French Responses
answered question		702	81	2	5	84
skipped question		128	6	0	7	17

Q7. If we asked the spouses of senior pastors or other leaders in your community if they felt that being married to a Christian leader had helped them grow in their love for Jesus, what do you think they would say? Why do you say that?

Answer Options	Response Percent	English Responses	Spanish Responses	Portugese Responses	Chinese Responses	French Responses
answered question		641	81	2	6	81
skipped question		189	6	0	6	20

Q8. A Zulu proverb says, "To lead is to die." It means that a leader does not get to live his own life anymore. Everyone will come to him to settle their problems. Many will criticize him for his decisions and these things never stop. How true is this in your experience of leadership?

Answer Options	Response Percent	English Responses	Spanish Responses	Portugese Responses	Chinese Responses	French Responses
Mostly or entirely true	45.2%	344	29	2	3	44
Sometimes true	48.5%	369	40	0	4	41
Rarely or never true	6.3%	48	10	0	1	0
Comments		486	65	2	3	64
	answered question	761	79	2	8	85
	skipped question	69	8	0	4	16

Q9. Suppose you are being called to a new ministry, but it does not start for another two years. You are being asked to hire someone now and mentor that person to take over when you leave. What are three of four of the most important things you will look for in this person?

Answer Options	Response Percent	English Responses	Spanish Responses	Portugese Responses	Chinese Responses	French Responses
answered question		694	80	2	6	85
skipped question		136	7	0	6	16

Q10. What would you say is the most frequent cause of failure in Christian leaders to "finish well" as a Christ-centered leader in the nation where you are currently living? (Check your top three from the list below.)

Answer Options	Response Percent	English Responses	Spanish Responses	Portugese Responses	Chinese Responses	French Responses
Inappropriate use of finances	32.8%	251	40	0	9	54
Family issues	25.2%	193	40	1	1	17
Sexual sin	32.9%	252	40	0	6	34
Lack of growth in their Christian life	37.5%	287	40	2	3	18
Inordinate pride	36.0%	276	45	0	0	32
Abuse of power	41.1%	315		0	6	39
Emotional/psychological wounding	22.2%	170		2	0	8
Burnout	40.1%	307	32	1	0	21
Lack of learning posture	21.3%	163	25	0	1	26
Comments		86	24	0	0	14
answered question		766	83	2	9	87
skipped question		64	4	0	3	14

Q11. Which answer comes the closest to explaining why there is such a shortage of Christ-centered leaders?

Answer Options	Response Percent	English Responses	Spanish Responses	Portugese Responses	Chinese Responses	French Responses
The current leaders won't allow the new ones to develop.	26.7%	173	21	0	4	18
The situations of leaders are so complicated and demanding that there simply aren't enough multitalented people to do them.	13.3%	86	3	0	2	3
So-called leadership training programs do not really prepare people to lead in the real world. People have credentials, but they can't lead.	40.6%	263	31	0	0	22
People appointing a new director prefer someone who is already the director or president of three or four other ministries to someone who could give them full time but is younger and less known.	10.2%	66	11	1	1	14
Churches are short of good leaders because they pay so little by comparison to NGOs and secular jobs.	9.1%	59	6	0	0	9
answered question		647	72	1	7	66
skipped question		183	15	1	5	35

Q12. Finish this sentence: Good leadership development will always...

Answer Options	Response Percent	English Responses	Spanish Responses	Portugese Responses	Chinese Responses	French Responses
answered question		561	72	1	5	52
skipped question		269	15	1	7	49

Q13. What has helped you grow in your abilities as a leader the most in the last five years? (Check your top three from the list below.)

Answer Options	Response Percent	English Responses	Spanish Responses	Portugese Responses	Chinese Responses	French Responses
Mentoring	54.5%	361	42	0	3	25
Classes	11.8%	78	11	0	2	38
Workshops	15.0%	99	14	0	5	12
Books	42.3%	280	25	1	3	34
Internet resources	5.6%	37	7	0	0	6
Small accountability group	29.3%	194	28	0	0	13
Feedback from your staff	28.5%	189	38	0	2	14
Informal discussions with peers	45.6%	302	23	1	2	25
Observing others	52.1%	345	30	0	4	37
Comments		128	16	1	0	6
answered question		662	76	1	7	67
skipped question		168	11	1	5	34

Q14. How well did your classroom studies prepare you to serve as a Christian leader?

Answer Options	Response Percent	English Responses	Spanish Responses	Portugese Responses	Chinese Responses	French Responses
Extremely well	6.4%	42	20	0	0	23
Well	30.3%	199	39	1	5	28
Somewhat	41.6%	273	14	0	2	14
Not very well	21.6%	142	4	0	0	2
answered question		656	77	1	7	67
skipped question		174	10	1	5	34

Q15. In what field(s) did you do enough classroom work to earn a diploma or degree? (Check all that apply.)

Answer Options	Response Percent	English Responses	Spanish Responses	Portugese Responses	Chinese Responses	French Responses
Bible/theology/mission/church history	58.4%	388	49	1	4	29
Business	18.5%	123	10	0	3	6
Education	23.8%	158	29	0	0	9
Medicine	13.1%	87	8	0	0	0
Law	2.4%	16	8	0	0	6
Social science	20.2%	134	15	0	1	14
Natural science	10.5%	70	4	0	2	2
Other (please specify)	24.4%	162	37	0	0	21
answered question		664	75	1	7	63
skipped question		166	12	1	5	38

Q16. The term "spiritual formation" is used to describe your growth as a disciple of Jesus. As a leader, do you feel that you are becoming more like Christ?

Answer Options	Response Percent	English Responses	Spanish Responses	Portugese Responses	Chinese Responses	French Responses
Yes, rapidly	3.9%	26	1	0	0	1
Yes, slow, but steady	54.4%	366	41	0	5	50
To some extent, but it seems to go forward for a while and then stop; then I grow some more	28.1%	189	23	0	1	10
Not to the extent I would like	12.9%	87	11	1	1	6
No, not really at all	0.7%	5	1	0	0	1
answered question		673	77	1	7	68
skipped question		157	10	1	5	33

Q17. If you believe you are growing and becoming more Christlike, what do you find has helped you grow the most in the last one to two years? (Check your top three from the list below.)

Answer Options	Response Percent	English Responses	Spanish Responses	Portugese Responses	Chinese Responses	French Responses
Prayer	57.0%	385	53	0	3	36
Fasting	6.8%	46	4	0	0	10
Bible study	50.8%	343	55	0	2	39
Fellowship with other believers	37.9%	256	24	0	3	25
Solitude	13.8%	93	6	0	1	1
Specific words from the Lord	15.6%	105	9	0	0	10
Rebukes or encouragements from friends	12.4%	84	6	0	1	9
Input from a mentor or older Christian friend	33.8%	228	26	0	3	18
Dreams and visions	4.1%	28	1	0	2	4
Failures	23.1%	156	13	0	4	10
Confession and repentance	16.0%	108	16	0	1	4
Meditation	12.1%	82	0	0	2	26
Submission	12.3%	83	0	0	0	5
Celebration	2.4%	16	0	0	0	0
Service	16.6%	112	19	0	2	8
Worship	16.7%	113	4	0	1	0
Not growing, does not apply	0.0%	0	0	0	0	0
Comments		64	7	0	7	3
answered question		675	76	0		68
skipped question		155	11	2	5	33

Q18. If you believe you are growing and becoming more Christlike, what do you find has consistently helped you grow as a disciple of Jesus throughout the years? (Check your top three from the list below.)

Answer Options	Response Percent	English Responses	Spanish Responses	Portugese Responses	Chinese Responses	French Responses
Prayer	59.3%	397	52	0	4	38
Fasting	4.9%	33	6	0	0	8
Bible study	71.4%	478	64	0	4	43
Fellowship with other believers	48.7%	326	24	0	2	26
Solitude	9.0%	60	4	0	0	4
Specific words from the Lord	13.2%	88	8	0	0	5
Rebukes or encouragements from friends	10.0%	67	4	0	0	4
Input (rebuke or encouragements from a mentor or older Christian friend)	27.4%	183	23	0	2	12
Dreams and visions	3.3%	22	3	0	1	2
Failures	14.3%	96	15	0	1	7
Confession and repentance	13.9%	93	13	0	0	6
Meditation	11.8%	79	9	0	3	21
Submission	7.6%	51	13	0	1	6
Celebration	1.8%	12	1	0	0	1
Service	14.1%	94	0	0	3	13
Worship	12.6%	84	5	0	0	0
Not growing, does not apply	0.1%	1	0	0	0	0
Comments		40	9	0	0	7
answered question		669	76	0	7	63
skipped question		161	11	2	5	38

Q19. Explain your answer for question eighteen further if you wish.

Answer Options	Response Percent	English Responses	Spanish Responses	Portugese Responses	Chinese Responses	French Responses
answered question		138	36	0	4	48
skipped question		692	51	2	8	53

Q20. If you had the opportunity to take classes in leadership development right now, what subjects would be of most interest to you? (Check your top three from the list below.)

Answer Options	Response Percent	English Responses	Spanish Responses	Portugese Responses	Chinese Responses	French Responses
Theological training	19.2%	128	24	0	3	15
Development and social change	22.0%	147	14	1	4	17
Ethics for leadership	19.2%	128	16	1	1	32
Mentoring/coaching	43.1%	288	30	0	5	10
Integrity and finance	9.1%	61	12	0	0	13
Fund-raising	6.4%	43	6	1	0	4
Conflict resolution	28.9%	193	26	0	1	31
Strategic planning	29.8%	199	22	0	2	22
People management	32.6%	218	9	0	0	25
Research for problem solving	7.6%	51	12	0	0	6
Computer skills	5.2%	35	11	0	1	14
Prayer and the personal life of a leader	40.7%	272	33	0	2	16
Spiritual formation	29.5%	197	19	0	2	0
Comments		41	5	0	0	4
answered question		668	77	1	7	67
skipped question		162	10	1	5	34

Q21. What types or forms of leadership development opportunities do you wish you had access to?

Answer Options	Response Percent	English Responses	Spanish Responses	Portugese Responses	Chinese Responses	French Responses
Mentoring	54.8%	343	38	1	6	28
Classes	14.1%	88	12	0	3	28
Workshops	29.1%	182	23	1	5	29
Books	18.5%	116	12	0	2	25
Feedback from staff	12.1%	76	25	0	0	6
Informal discussion with peers	32.7%	205	21	0	2	21
Internet resources	12.8%	80	17	1	0	24
Small accountability group	38.0%	238	20	0	5	20
Observing others	19.3%	121	16	0	3	12
None at this time	8.5%	53	5	0	0	0
Comments		45	8		0	5
answered question		626	77	1	7	66
skipped question		204	10	1	5	35

Q22. Finish this sentence, "Our churches and our nation would be much better off today if all Christians in positions of leadership were a lot more..."

Answer Options	Response Percent	English Responses	Spanish Responses	Portugese Responses	Chinese Responses	French Responses
answered question		598	74	1	5	57
skipped question		232	13	1	7	44

Q23. How is your concept of Christian leadership different now than it was ten or twenty years ago? Can you briefly say what caused it to change?

Answer Options	Response Percent	English Responses	Spanish Responses	Portugese Responses	Chinese Responses	French Responses
answered question		503	75	1	5	57
skipped question		327	12	1	7	44

Q24. From the list below choose up to five of the most pressing issues facing Christian leaders in your nation.

Answer Options	Response Percent	English Responses	Spanish Responses	Portugese Responses	Chinese Responses	French Responses
Ethnic conflict	27.5%	180	8	0	3	29
Integrity	72.5%	474	70	1	3	33
Religious conflict	34.7%	227	18	1	0	23
Personal pride	75.7%	495	65	1	7	40
Poverty	26.5%	173	40	0	0	51
Spiritual warfare	50.8%	332	18	0	3	26
Lack of infrastructure (training)	31.8%	208	40	1	6	50
Political instability	9.9%	65	6	0	1	23
Corruption	33.8%	221	44	1	4	41
Comments		124	17	0	0	5
answered question		654	77	1	7	66
skipped question		176	10	1	5	35

Q25. Some leaders claim that the affirmation from a more mature leader greatly helped them become better leaders.

Answer Options	Response Percent	English Responses	Spanish Responses	Portugese Responses	Chinese Responses	French Responses
In general, has this been true in your case?	99.2%	592	73	1	5	49
If yes, how many leaders helped to develop you in this way?	91.5%	546	61	1	5	45
answered question		597	74	1	5	51
skipped question		233	13	1	7	50

Q26. Please share one specific thing that a more mature leader did that greatly encouraged/affirmed you to help you become who you are today.

Answer Options	Response Percent	English Responses	Spanish Responses	Portugese Responses	Chinese Responses	French Responses
answered question		556	71	1	4	58
skipped question		274	16	1	8	43

Q27. Please tell us you age. (Check one.)

Answer Options	Response Percent	English Responses	Spanish Responses	Portugese Responses	Chinese Responses	French Responses
Under 30	5.9%	40	9	0	1	2
30–40	23.2%	158	14	0	5	26
40–50	22.5%	153	30	1	1	25
50–60	32.7%	223	17	0	0	8
Over 60	15.7%	107	7	0	0	0
answered question		681	77	1	7	61
skipped question		149	10	1	5	40

Q28. Sex

Answer Options	Response Percent	English Responses	Spanish Responses	Portugese Responses	Chinese Responses	French Responses
Male	68.5%	463	43	1	4	57
Female	31.5%	213	33	0	2	5
answered question		676	76	1	6	62
skipped question		154	11	1	6	39

Q29. Please tell us which leadership position best describes your current primary role. (Check one ONLY.)

Answer Options	Response Percent	English Responses	Spanish Responses	Portugese Responses	Chinese Responses	French Responses
Business leader	5.0%	31	2	0	0	3
Professional	16.3%	101	10	0	1	5
Political leader	0.5%	3	0	0	0	0
Church leader	18.7%	116	11	0	0	9
Pastor	21.6%	134	17	1	3	14
NGO, mission agency, or development agency leader	28.3%	175	21	0	2	16
No formal leadership role currently	9.5%	59	0	0	0	0
Comments		94	16	0	0	14
answered question		619	77	1	6	61
skipped question		211	10	1	6	40